FINDING
EACH OTHER

*A Practical Guide to Achieving
Successful Relationships*

By the same author
THE VISUAL HANDBOOK

FINDING EACH OTHER

A Practical Guide to Achieving Successful Relationships

John Selby

Element Books

First published in Great Britain 1987 by
Element Books Limited,
Longmead, Shaftesbury, Dorset

Designed by Jenny Liddle

Cover illustration by John King

Photographs by Birgitta Steiner and Budd Smith

Printed and bound in Great Britain by
Billings, Hylton Road, Worcester

British Library Cataloguing in Publication Data
Selby, John
Finding each other : a practical guide
to achieving successful relationships.
1. Interpersonal relations
I. Title II. Einander Finden. *English*
158'.2 HM132

ISBN 1-85230-019-1

CONTENTS

PART SIX:

JOHN SELBY, a graduate of Princeton University, the University of California, and the Graduate Theological Union, is a psychologist and author working both in the United States and in Europe. The author of seven previous books on interpersonal relating, perception, healing techniques, and fiction, Selby has travelled in Mexico, Guatemala, South Africa, and Hawaii, exploring native approaches to emotional health, social interaction, and hunting techniques.

Born in 1945 in California, Selby was raised on the Papago Indian reservation in southern Arizona until he was nine. With this background, he has worked professionally to incorporate native understandings into the contemporary psychological and sociological approaches to therapy and interpersonal education.

Once a champion fencer, Selby has also worked to include the hunting and martial arts traditions into the formal structure of therapy techniques, employing zen, tantric and various native approaches to developing a client's sense of personal power and expanded awareness.

Beginning his professional career in the therapy tradition of Wilhelm Reich and Fritz Perls, Selby held research positions at the New Jersey Neuro-psychiatric Institute, the Bureau of Research in Neurology and Psychiatry, and the American Institute for Mental Health. He has also developed health programmes for the American Airline Pilots Association, Aetna Life Insurance, and Apple and IBM Computers.

He recently has focused on the writing of three new books, while continuing with research and lecturing in Europe and America.

For two people to find each
other they should first find themselves.
Then the finding of each other
comes quickly.

Papago Indian proverb

INTRODUCTION

We all know people who seem to be blessed with a magic charm when it comes to meeting the right people to fulfil their various interpersonal needs. Almost always, they are in the company of friends who love them, who accept them as they are and eagerly interact with them to their mutual satisfaction.

Whenever these lucky people develop interpersonal needs which are not being satisfied by their present circle of friends and associates, they are able actively to seek out a new person to fulfil those needs. In fact, their lives seem to be blessed with a magic ability to attract the right people to their doorsteps.

But is it really simple luck which determines our success in finding the right people we need in our lives? Are some of us born with a natural attraction which brings us friends, lovers, and partners, while others must accept a fate of frustration and unsatisfied interpersonal desires? What are the hidden factors which determine success or failure in finding each other?

As a therapist working regularly with clients who are struggling with this problem of establishing satisfying relationships, I have been exploring this particular question during the past two decades, searching along with my colleagues for more effective ways to help people resolve their unfulfilled interpersonal needs.

We have taken a close look both at the lucky people, and in contrast at the seemingly unlucky people, trying to gain a broader insight into the workings of interpersonal encounter. What we have found is that there are definite factors in the lucky person's approach to fulfilling his or her needs, factors which are being overlooked by the frustrated, lonely people who do not succeed in finding new friends and partners.

In fact, the lucky people, who seem effortlessly to resolve their interpersonal needs, are actually, upon closer observation, making very definite steps from the time they realize they have an unfulfilled need to the time they establish a new relationship which satisfies that need; and conversely, people with difficulties establishing satisfying relationships are those who are, for one reason or another, not able to make one or more of the steps that lead to a successful encounter. There appear to be six primary steps in this process of finding each other, and each step must be consciously or unconsciously fulfilled for the process to end in a satisfying friendship or professional relationship.

The first factor in fulfilling an interpersonal need is quite obvious, but all too often completely overlooked. Many of us feel a general yearning, or a deep frustration in our interpersonal relationships, but we fail to gain a clear understanding of the nature of that yearning. We struggle blindly to find someone to relieve our need, but we fail because we haven't clarified the specific requirements and qualities of our yearning or frustration. In short, there is a lack of mental reflection and clarity.

The second factor deals not with our mental clarity, but with our emotional clarity. Most of us carry with us from our childhood various inhibitions when it comes to relating with other people. All too often, these inhibitions block our successful expression of our needs, and hold us back from acting to gain fulfilment. So emotional growth beyond old inhibitions is a necessary step to consider, in the process of finding each other.

The third factor has to do with our general readiness for a relationship. All too often, the right people meet each other at the wrong time, before they are ready to succeed with their friendship, and the friendship fails as a result. Positive, expanding relationships exist only when both partners have developed their own personal strengths and emotional maturity.

The fourth factor appears, on first viewing, actually to be a matter of magic. Most of us have experienced at least once 'a chance encounter' with someone, a 'purely coincidental' meeting which developed into a deep friendship, professional partnership, or romantic involvement; and our folklore is full of tales of the mystic forces which bring two lovers together. In fact, most people feel that there are spiritual dimensions in life which act to guide people to fated encounters.

This dimension of 'finding each other' has fascinated me for years, both in my own life, and in the lives of my friends and clients. How is it that two people who are looking for a special partner can suddenly turn a corner, look into each other's eyes, and recognize that they have found each other?

The new physics begun by Albert Einstein has given us a new insight into the dynamics of such 'chance encounters'. In the understanding of quantum mechanics, for instance, the conscious mind is definitely considered an active factor in what happens in the physical world. Consciousness is a force which affects material functioning, and therefore, the focusing of one's attention clearly upon one's interpersonal need could in fact help attract a person of 'like mind'.

Especially when we consider that there are always at least two people needed for an encounter to take place, the suggestions of the new physics become quite fascinating. When two people with similar needs and compatible personalities are both actively looking for each other, a polarity between them can develop, which could help bring them together.

So in considering the steps to successful encounters between two people, we should consider this dimension of mutual attraction between two people, even before they have their first encounter. There are, in fact, potent meditations which serve to augment this attraction. Some of my more conservative colleagues have shied away from working with this fourth factor in helping people resolve their interpersonal needs. But I find this dimension essential in a complete programme for 'finding each other'. Learning how to expand our consciousness so that life has more 'magic' to it is something we all desire, and I have found this dimension especially effective with clients who have put it to work on practical levels, while also dealing with the more mundane aspects of 'finding each other'.

The fifth factor in 'finding each other' returns to a more

pragmatic level, that of the actual encounter of two people for the first time. Unfortunately, even if the right people meet each other, the encounter can fail if certain aspects are not clearly understood. The moment of encounter with a special person can be intense, and often throws us off-balance. We lose our mental clarity and become blocked right when we should act.

So preparation for the desired encounter is an important fifth step in our 'finding each other' process. Right when we have found what we have been looking for, we must be especially centred and confident, or we can lose the friend just when the friendship has hardly begun.

The sixth factor deals with the successful development of relationships, after the first encounter has taken place. Many people have luck in finding people to relate with initially, but make the same mistakes over and over again during the first weeks and months of the relationship. Eventually the friendship or partnership falls apart, and the person must start all over again, looking for a new person.

So a pragmatic look at the pitfalls in relationships and a deeper understanding of how relationships grow is the final factor to be considered.

My intention in writing this book, has been to explore with you these six factors. Also, and perhaps more importantly, I want to offer to you the various programmes my colleagues and I have developed, to help you succeed with each step, so you do attain your goal of 'finding each other'.

In Part One you will find a discussion of the most important questions you should ask yourself, in order to evaluate your needs, hungers, desires and yearnings, so that you can clearly understand what you need in life and how you can best satisfy that need. Hopefully, by the time you finish this discussion, you will know what you really need in a new relationship, know your readiness to fulfil that need, and know in what directions to look for such fulfilment.

In Part Two, we will assess your emotional readiness for the desired encounter and relationship, and also establish whether you are still carrying with you certain childhood inhibitions which can seriously interfere with any movement towards finding the desired person. All of us have anxieties and uncertainties when it comes to relating with other people, and this section of the book will offer the basic programme which I use with clients in moving beyond such blocks.

Part Three is very positive in nature, in that it offers a programme for self-enhancement, for the development of inner strength and beauty. We will explore your inner ability to satisfy many of your deeper needs, so that you will not appear so 'needy' in your relating with other people. If you first develop a dynamic, positive, expansive feeling inside yourself, you will find your ability to attract others to you greatly enhanced. This preparation for encounter is fulfilling in itself, in that you discover how to be your own best friend.

Part Four moves into the magic of encounter. We assume that, for you to meet someone at some time in the future, that person must already, in the present, exist. Furthermore, that person is right now moving towards an encounter with you. So you can learn to focus your attention, through various meditation techniques, to help attract that special person out there to you. If you are lucky, that person is also reading this book, and practising the same meditations for encountering you.

Along with this more esoteric dimension of Part Four, we will also explore the pragmatic aspects of the search for a new partner or friend. For instance, if you have perceptual habits of 'not looking', of avoiding eye contact, you will block any encounter; and if you are projecting an ideal image on every face you encounter, rather than looking to see the real people out there, you will also interfere with recognizing the actual person you are looking for.

Another factor we will consider will be your habits of movement. If you are sitting alone most of the time in your home, not actively putting yourself in positions where you could meet someone, you are directly blocking the very experience you desire. Movement itself is essential to fulfilling any desire, and breaking free of the lack of movement patterns so many of us have

5

developed is a key to the success of this over-all programme. The movement exercises are also quite a pleasure to do in themselves!

A final aspect of Part Four has to do with timing. One of our great problems when we have an unfulfilled need or desire is impatience. Unfortunately, when we are impatient, unwilling to flow with the natural movement of time, we interfere with the entire process of 'finding each other', So learning to remain in the present moment, rather than always pushing into the future, is a vital aspect of this programme. Enjoyment of the present is in fact a key to fulfilment in the future.

Part Five deals with the intensity of meeting an exciting person in your life. Knowing how to breathe into this new experience, rather than automatically contracting away from the intensity, is invaluable at the moment of encounter.

Exercises in maintaining our own centre, especially when we 'fall in love', are vital. To lose our centre in another person, to go unconscious right when we need to be extra aware, is quite dangerous.

Honesty is another factor to consider in the first moments, hours, and days of a new friendship. We tend to want to paint ourselves in a good light so that we will be accepted; but for a successful long-term relationship, we simply need to relax and be ourselves, even if that means being rejected. Perhaps this person is not the right one after all. Honesty is the guiding force to finding the right person, and we can actively develop our ability to remain honest at crucial moments.

In Part Six we will explore the various pitfalls which friends and couples, partners and colleagues, encounter along the path of relationships. Dependency, possessiveness, the need for private space, the problems of personal growth and unsatisfied needs in a relationship, will all be considered, as well as the positive ways to augment a relationship through shared experiences.

So now you have a brief over-view of the discussion and programmes which follow. I hope that this book can serve as a manual in all the different types of relationsips you will need in the years to come, so that you can most fully satisfy your potential for loving, creating, communicating, and surviving to your utmost!

PART ONE
Clarifying Your Specific Needs and Requirements

Perhaps the greatest challenge for most of us, in our movement towards establishing a new and satisfying relationship, is that of gaining mental clarity regarding our emotional needs.

When we hunger for a new lover, for instance, we are usually consumed with the emotions of passion, sexual desire, longing, and excitement. Clear thinking is very difficult in the face of intense emotions. In fact, the thinking part of our brain is quite separate from the older, more primitive emotional centres of the brain, and the more we are caught in an emotional need or hunger, the less ability we have to pause and think through our present situation.

So as a beginning we should go through a process which I use regularly with my clients, to clarify your present needs and desires, and to see what practical steps you need to make in order to satisfy your yearnings and interpersonal requirements.

First of all, at a basic level, what is the nature of your need? Consider the list below, and determine what general category your need fits into. If more than one category applies, decide which categories are more important to you, and which are secondary:

BASIC NEEDS
1. primary survival　　　　　　　_____
2. business help　　　　　　　　_____
3. sexual release　　　　　　　　_____
4. intimacy　　　　　　　　　　_____
5. family security　　　　　　　_____
6. emotional growth　　　　　　_____
7. spiritual growth　　　　　　　_____
8. friendship　　　　　　　　　_____

If you want, you can say to yourself, before the words in each category, 'I need a new person in my life, primarily for . . .' and see which category or categories seems most dominant for you.

To go a step further, there are twelve important questions which you will want to reflect upon in depth.

1. Where in your body, right now, do you feel the presence of your specific need or yearning?

All of our emotions are actual feelings in our bodies. Close your eyes a moment, watch your breathing, and feel where your need seems to be centred in your body.

2. For how long have you felt this need in your body?

Is this an old yearning which dates back to childhood, or is it a new feeling? Reflect a moment, allow your memory to take you back, as you continue to feel the need in your body, and explore the sources of this need.

3. What is required for this need to be satisfied?

Take a step back from the actual feeling in your body now, and allow your mind to think clearly about the actual ways in which this need you feel could be satisfied. Make a list if you want to; very often, making lists helps in gaining mental clarity. Exactly what do you require, in order to relieve this hunger you feel inside you?

4. In your past, has this need ever been satisfied by someone?

To gain a deeper perspective, see what memories effortlessly rise to the surface now, as you take a few moments and see who in your past has relieved this feeling inside you. Explore whatever memories come, and perhaps you will discover some unseen blocks to future relating, which were generated by painful experiences in the past. Just be honest with yourself.

5. Are you ready to meet a person who could satisfy your present need?

Again, honesty with yourself is the key to clarity. See what your feelings tell you, when you allow them to speak. Are you ready to open yourself to a new encounter, or are you still needing to heal somewhere inside your emotional skin?

6. Could you perhaps satisfy this need yourself?

Curiously, many of the needs we feel, and which we want someone to satisfy, are needs we can take care of ourselves. In fact, once we leave the intimacy of our mothers, there are certain basic needs which no new person can satisfy; we must become our own best friend and give ourselves the love and acceptance our mothers once gave us. So consider for a moment to what extent you love yourself and give yourself fulfilment.

7.   What particular qualities do you need in a person in order to find satisfaction?

Begin to clarify exactly what qualities you are looking for in a person; what, honestly, do you need to feel satisfied? Make a list if you want to expand your mental clarity.

8.   What particular qualities in a person inhibit your fulfilment of your interpersonal need?

Let the negative part of your mind come into play now, and bring into consciousness the judging part of your mind. It is essential to see how your eyes judge another person, how your mind separates 'positive' encounters from the more 'negative' ones. Through becoming aware of your likes and dislikes, you clarify the nature of your needs.

9.   Are you frightened of letting the outside world know about your need?

All too often, our parents and childhood educators put a negative judgement on some of our basic needs in life. Especially when it came to sexual hungers, most of us were punished for open expression of our needs for intimacy. We therefore have a fear of showing anyone our needs. Look to yourself now, and to the need we are focusing upon. See if you can honestly let the world know that you have this need, or if you feel guilty for having such a need.

10.   Are you frightened to find someone who could satisfy your need?

If we have fear attached to our desires, we put great blocks between us and those who could satisfy us. If you feel such a fear, the best beginning approach is simply to begin looking at that fear, face it directly, get to know it. You can move a great distance with this simple exercise of watching your breathing right now, feeling your desire or need, and imagining meeting someone who would like to fulfil your need or hunger. Accept the feelings which rise up, and continue to breathe into them, to get to know them. You will notice that they begin to change as you hold your attention to them, and you have found a technique for emotional growth!

11.   Are you being honest with yourself right now?

We often have great mental tricks we play on ourselves, in order to avoid painful or frightening thoughts or realizations. Once again, the best way to begin to change these habits is to watch them in action! Just take a good breath and look to see if you have considered these questions honestly or not. Accept whatever you find in yourself.

12.   Can you think of a simple action you could take, today, which would move you in the direction of fulfilling your need?

Inability to act in the proper direction is a primary factor which blocks the fulfilment of your desires and yearnings. So right now in the beginning of this programme, you should begin to encourage your mind to think of a simple step you could make, to move in the desired directions. This mental act, which is aimed at encouraging movement, is vital to fulfilment of any need.

TALKING WITH A FRIEND

As an example of what you could do actively to begin your movement towards a new relationship, I will offer a common beginning point I suggest for clients.

Consider the people you know, and see if one of them would be willing to listen to you talk for just half an hour about your present situation.

If you have such a friend, get together, honestly tell him or her about this programme, and your interpersonal need, and then go through the above twelve questions with your friend. This process of expressing your feelings to another person can be dramatically helpful in opening yourself to a new encounter. Perhaps you will want to trade places with your friend at some point, and be the listener as he or she works through a frustration.

These twelve questions should serve as a solid base from which you can grow towards finding each other. You will want to reflect upon them a number of times, in different moods, to gain their full effect. In fact, I often have clients review their feelings towards these questions once a day, for ten days. I ask them to look at the first question, to breathe consciously for four breath cycles, and then see what thoughts, memories, images or emotions come to mind, before going on to the next question. You might do the same.

1. Where in your body, right now, do you feel the presence of your specific need or yearning?
2. For how long have you felt this need in your body?
3. What is required for this need to be satisfied?
4. In your past, has this need ever been satisfied by someone?
5. Are you ready to meet a person who could satisfy your need?
6. Could you perhaps satisfy this need yourself?
7. What particular qualities do you need in a person?
8. What particular qualities in a person would inhibit your fulfilment of your interpersonal need?
9. Are you afraid to let the outside world know of your need?
10. Are you frightened to find someone who could satisfy you?
11. Are you being honest with yourself right now?
12. Can you think of an action you could take today, which would move you towards fulfilling your need?

WHAT YOU HAVE TO OFFER OTHERS

We have just explored what you want from someone else. Now we need to turn around and do just the opposite, to be clear what you are willing to give, in exchange for what you want to receive. Only when there is a balance between the giving and the taking do relationships work. Too often, we are so focused on satisfying our own needs, we fail to remember that relationships require as much giving as taking. Simple mental focusing on this dimension begins to open your potential for giving.

First of all, are you looking for a person out there who is like you, with weaknesses and needs, faults and desires, emotional wounds and mental blind-spots? Or are you expecting to find someone who is perfect, who has no problems, who can take you on and help you without demanding anything in return?

This might seem like a foolish question, but it is in fact a very common stumbling block for people. As children, we all had our visions of white knights and fairy princesses, who existed in a realm beyond ours, and who would come to us and comfort us. Are you still waiting for such a magical encounter, or are you now realistic about our life situation, where our needs are satisfied only by people who are also in need?

Just pause and reflect, see what you find when you take a deep breath and are honest with yourself. When you discover old expectations and fantasies that are still alive, just see them with a sense of humour, and give them room and love to grow.

We can go a step further with this question of your ideal image of a friend, sexual partner or mate. Are you looking for someone who is your equal, or someone who is beyond you in emotional health and maturity?

As funny as it might seem, many people are seeking for a perfect beauty or handsome champion to share their life with, whereas in practical reality, such a peson certainly would not choose as a partner someone as normal and full of struggles as we are. So if you are honest, would the man or woman of your dreams really choose you as a partner?

This brings us to the question of equality. Relationships only work when there is a feeling of mutual equality between the partners. You must attract someone similar to you, in order for your needs to be satisfied. Is the image of the person you are seeking similar to your own personality and level of development? Just pause a moment and contemplate this question.

We all developed ideal images in our minds as we were growing up. Very often these ideal images stand in the way of our meeting people who can satisfy our needs, because we are looking for someone who does not exist. Our willingness to give up these ideal images and dreams determines our readiness to find a real person with whom to satisfy our real needs and desires.

Now, we can look directly at what you have to offer another person in a relationship. To what extent are you willing to give of yourself, to help satisfy another person's needs? Please be acutely honest with yourself here, rather than painting a pretty picture of your ability to give.

I am willing and able to give:

1. friendship _____
2. intimacy _____
3. financial support _____
4. fun and laughter _____
5. emotional warmth _____
6. sexual fulfilment _____
7. spiritual comfort _____
8. acceptance _____

With each category, you might read the word, then close your eyes, be aware of your breathing, and see what spontaneous thoughts or feelings come to you.

If there are categories where you are not willing to give to a person, let yourself accept this for now. We all have areas where it is easy to give, and areas where we need help in learning to give.

SEEING YOURSELF

So far in this discussion we have been playing regularly with your ability to take a good look at yourself, to see what you feel inside your body, to explore your inner worlds of thoughts, images and sensations, and to evaluate your present inner experience.

This ability to turn your inner vision to watch yourself, without judgement of what you see, is one of the primary growth-oriented techniques that my colleagues and I have been working with, in helping people grow rapidly through emotional blocks and contractions of consciousness.

I would like to point out, without further hesitation, that this ability to see yourself is a learned ability. This means that you can develop the ability through regular practice of particular exercises. So if you are feeling frustrated with some of the exercises, I want to mention that most people need some practice before they can fully turn their attention inward, to watch their breathing, and to allow whatever thoughts and images come to mind.

Perhaps one of the most important realizations of modern psychology has been that the simple seeing of a negative habit, the simple observation of a constricted breathing pattern or the simple realization of a negative thought habit generates its own movement towards emotional health. Every time we expand our awareness to see ourselves more clearly, we create an opportunity for a movement beyond our old habits.

Every time you return to the questions presented in this first chapter, you will find that you see yourself in a new light. You will see your consciousness evolving, through pausing regularly and looking. These questions in this chapter, as well as in the next, are actually windows through which you can watch yourself growing. So I recommend that you set aside time to return to the questions, to practise regularly this art of looking inward, and to stimulate new growth through further looking in these special directions.

PART TWO
Emotional Growth and Healing

When I was first thinking of writing this book, I had several discussions with prominent editors. One of them told me bluntly that there would not be a large market for the book I had in mind. He said that it was true, at least half of us are unsatisfied with our present level of relationships, and we could all use some pointers on how to expand our ability to meet the right people in our lives.

But he said that on the opposite front, almost no one really wants to make an effort to grow, to push beyond old habits which inhibit our movement towards desired encounters. He was especially negative about this particular chapter — he felt that very few people, picking up this book, would be interested in a chapter on emotional growth. They would want tips on how to get out and find exciting people — they would not want tips on how to stay home and work through old emotional wounds.

Obviously, I did not decide to publish this book through that editor. I decided, on the contrary, that I had a much higher regard for the average reader than he did, and my experience has proven me true. People do seem to accept the challenge of this chapter. They do want some guidelines on how to move beyond old emotional blocks, and they are willing to face themselves honestly, evaluate their weak spots, and push through old inhibitions towards future fulfilment.

So I am writing this chapter not with an eye to the publishing market, but simply as a therapist who has seen the stumbling blocks people encounter in fulfilling their needs, and who knows at least some of the practical techniques you can use to overcome those stumbling blocks. I am not promising instant success; I am offering realistic steps you can make, if you need to, towards emotional healing and positive changes in habits.

First of all, let's take a very quick look at the nature of needs.

You are obviously quite successful in meeting most of your human needs. When you are hungry, and feel the need for food, you manage to obtain food, and to put it in your mouth, and digest it. When you feel cold, you feel the need to cover your body, and you are quite successful in doing this. You also manage to satisfy the human need for shelter, to keep a roof over your head. Like all animals, our needs are responses of our bodies when our survival is threatened, and like all animals, we have developed complex means of satisfying our basic needs.

But when it comes to our social needs, to our needs for intimacy, companionship, verbal as well as sexual intercourse, human beings, especially these days, have a considerably more difficult time in meeting needs and hungers than do other life forms on the planet.

Rather than write a long dissertation on the psychology of human needs and hungers, I will instead offer you a few key questions to ponder, so you can see how your own childhood affected your ability to reach out and ask the world for what you need emotionally.

As a beginning, consider:

1. Did your parents allow you to express your basic need directly, to show your emotions openly, and to be spontaneous in your emotional expression?

   (You can pause and see what memories about your childhood might come back. See if you can remember the feeling in your body when you were with your parents. See how your breathing felt. Notice if you were afraid to run and shout, to let your emotions flow freely.)

2. Was there a general inhibition regarding sexuality in your home and community?

   (If your parents and teachers, church and friends were frightened of expressing their sexual needs, you certainly picked up this fear also.)

3. Were you brought up to think of others before yourself, to

avoid being selfish, and to give more than you received?

(Especially in religious upbringings, children feel guilty for hungering for their own satisfaction, and this guilt then contaminates their movement towards seeking satisfaction of basic needs and yearnings.)

4. Do you find that your breathing becomes tight and shallow when you are in certain social situations?

(Our breathing is the basic indicator of our emotions. If you begin to watch your breathing, you will find that you have habits of breathing which directly inhibit your ability to express yourself, and to reach out for what you desire.)

5. When you feel strongly a need in your body, do you have a fear reaction, a feeling of anxiety related to the feeling of desire?

(This linking of fear with desire is a primary learned reaction which blocks our movement towards satisfaction in relationships. Old unconscious fears stand like walls between us and satisfaction. We will consider direct programmes which help one recover from such fear reactions.)

6. Were you taught to postpone gratification of your desires, in order to receive rewards in some future time?

(Our modern culture thrives on this future-oriented channelling of basic desires. Unfortunately, when we are always looking to the future for satisfaction, we never attain satisfaction. This is because, obviously, satisfaction of a need only occurs in the present moment. So the basic habit of living for the future eliminates our opportunities of satisfaction in the present moment.)

7. Have past experiences in your life conditioned you to expect negative punishment when you reach out to fulfil your basic needs?

(We are certainly conditioned by experience. Only when we become conscious of this past conditioning can we begin to move beyond it. Many of us are frozen, unable to act to satisfy our desires, because we expect a hit on the head when we do act. Learning to risk acting in the present moment is a major step beyond this conditioning.)

As with the questions in the first chapter, these new questions are effective when considered a number of times. At first, you give a shallow reaction to the questions, but as you return to them, you will find that your unconscious mind has been busy with the questions, and new insights will pop to the surface of your mind. So again, I recommend that you return to these questions at least half a dozen times, so that you have fully explored your relationship with each.

From these basic questions, we can conclude the following:
1. that children are often punished for expressing their basic, and quite natural, needs and desires;
2. that children develop fears associated with various natural desires and yearnings, when repeatedly punished for expressing those needs;
3. that religious training always to put yourself last leads to a feeling of guilt when you want to act directly to satisfy your own needs and hungers;
4. that always looking to the future leads to a frustration of satisfaction in the present;
5. that we are often victims of our past conditioning, unless we consciously act to transform old habits into more satisfying ones;
6. that our breathing is a direct link to our old habits, and that through working with our breathing, we can therefore begin to alter our anxiety patterns and move beyond old fear reactions.

In fact, fear is the great inhibition which we need to deal with if we are to act successfully to satisfy our interpersonal needs. Fear freezes us from action. And we cannot move, we are basically unable to relate at all, let alone relate in the ways that most satisfy us.

If fear is the primary blocking agent, what is the primary agent for reversing that block? Movement! If you are sitting down and realize you are hungry, you must go through a particular process of movement in order to get up and find yourself something to eat.

Likewise, if you are in need of finding someone to relate with, you must get up and move towards other people.

Movement and breathing, I am sure you realize, are directly linked with each other, at a basic biological level. For every movement you make, there is a breathing pattern which comes along with it, to keep your oxygen supply at a proper level in your bloodstream.

Also, for every emotion there is a related breathing pattern which enables you to express your feelings, through vocalization and movement. For instance, if you feel a need, and cannot attain that need, you become frustrated, or angry. Anger is a particular, powerful breathing pattern, which prepares us to shout for attention, or to act forcefully to obtain what we need.

Fear, conversely, which comes if you are punished for acting forcefully, is a blocking of the breathing. If your breathing is blocked, then you have no power, and thus you will not act in ways that bring about punishment.

This is the essence of fear — a blocked breathing pattern which inhibits action, which especially inhibits your natural action towards satisfying your needs and desires.

So we need to consider whether your breathing is inhibited as a habit, or free to express your emotions. Watch your breathing right now. Is it tight in your chest or deep in your belly? Is it full and smooth, or do you tend to hold your breath often? Can you exhale powerfully to feel your power, or is your exhalation blocked through tension in the diaphragm muscle?

Just begin to become aware of your breathing, moment to moment, and you will find that, when you begin to think about a need which is not satisfied, your breathing becomes affected. Simply notice, first of all, the relationship between your breathing and your interpersonal needs and desires. Get to know yourself better at this level.

When people have difficulties establishing satisfying relationships as adults, we can usually return to their early-childhood relationships, especially with their parents, and find difficulties which still need to be resolved before new relationships can be established. You can find out quickly for yourself whether this applies to you, through considering again that first list of needs which we explored in Part One.

This time, however, we should consider whether your mother and father satisfied your primary needs when you were young. Take your mother first, and see how she fulfilled your needs:

1. primary survival needs
2. needs for intimacy
3. family security
4. emotional comfort
5. spiritual growth
6. friendship
7. trust
8. acceptance

In which categories did your mother satisfy your basic needs, and in which do you feel she did not satisfy you? This is not a judgement against or for your mother, but simply a means of understanding your present emotional condition.

Now go down the list with your father, and see if your needs were satisfied, or frustrated, in your relationship with him. Breathe, relax, and see what comes to mind as you give each

23

category two breaths, to see your emotional reaction to each word related to your father.

Now, considering the categories where your needs were not well satisfied as an infant and young child, compare them with your present-day list of unsatisfied needs.

If you find that your present-day frustrations are the same as your infant and childhood frustrations, then you can see that, somehow, you are still holding on to those old frustrations, that perhaps you don't think you can ever be satisfied in certain ways, and so you don't even try.

In fact, people do recover from such childhood frustrations. First, you must admit that you did not receive full satisfaction as a child. Then you must imagine talking with your parents, and tell them how you feel about their not satisfying your needs. Once you have discharged this emotional pressure, once you have at least in your fantasy expressed your frustration, anger, whatever, to them, you can begin to let go of that deep desire to have them give you something they didn't. And once you stop expecting anyone to give you what you didn't receive in childhood, you are free to open yourself to what new experiences you can have with new intimates.

We can never regain something we did not get in the past. We can only let go of those resentments and frustrations, and allow ourselves to be satisfied, as adults with our adult needs, in the present. This is a point which cannot be expressed too often.

I would also recommend that you play another fantasy game with yourself, to clarify how your needs were satisfied as a child. Simply pause and allow a face from your childhood to come to mind. Imagine looking at that face to see what needs that person satisfied in you. Then, if that person is no longer alive, or no longer satisfying that need for you, consciously accept that this bond has been lost, and that you must look elsewhere for a similar relationship.

All too often, when someone is suddenly gone from our lives, we do not fully go through the mourning process. If a grandmother dies, we don't fully let go of her, we don't fully accept that she is no longer present to satisfy our basic emotional needs. So we remain in limbo, unable to let go of that emotional attachment, and therefore unable to open ourselves to a replacement relationship.

This is also true when a love affair breaks up, or when a friendship comes apart. We continue to look towards the lost lover for our deepest intimate support, rather than accepting that the person is gone, and that we must let go, recover, and move forward in life to a new relationship.

Visualize such a person's face a moment, and tell this person how you feel about them taking their love away from you. See what words come to mind, and actually say them aloud if you can. And then let them say what they might say back to you. Go through this dialogue a number of times, until you feel adequately free of this person. Of course, letting go of someone takes time, so give yourself time.

You can also simply watch how your breathing changes when you sit down and allow old faces of relatives and friends to come to mind. Becoming conscious of how your breathing is altered through your consideration of this relationship with different people provides insights that can prove invaluable in the present.

By bringing these old relationships to the surface of your awareness, you can begin to see how you project old expectations onto new relationships, thereby often destroying the actual, unique relationship that might have developed.

This attempt to regain old relationships through new people is one of the primary factors in unsatisfactory relating. In fact, we can never regain anything that was in the past. The past is just a goodbye. If you cannot say goodbye to the past, you cannot say hello to the new present. Certainly, memories linger; but to depend on old feelings and relationships to satisfy interpersonal needs in the present is simply not going to work.

So spend some time reflecting, doing these visualization exercises drawn from the Gestalt therapy tradition. Allow your self to work through unfinished business with past relationships, so you can be more free to relate in the present. Verbalize the feelings which arise, so that you can more effectively discharge old pressures and buried emotions.

In the next section, the basic movement/breathing/personal power exercises which are presented will also prove very effective in emotional growth.

Now we should consider your present emotional condition. In the list below, evaluate your feelings right now, and see which category most applies to your emotional state:

"I feel ... "
1. depressed ...
2. happy ...
3. angry ...
4. sad ...
5. frustrated ...
6. excited ...
7. anxious ...
8. empty ...

Notice what breathing pattern seems to reflect how you feel. Consider how often you feel this way. When you do not feel this way, what is the next most common feeling?

Now, let's play with some unfinished sentences to which you provide the ending. This is a means of helping you clarify your feelings towards relationships:

1. "When I think of my present life, I feel ... "
2. "When I think about my childhood, my basic feeling is one of ..."
3. "If I imagine meeting someone I really like, I feel my breathing becoming ... "
4. "I wish my mother had ... me more."
5. "Sometimes, I feel like just ... "
6. "When I think about meeting someone who really satisfies me, I feel ... "

Now, after reading this paragraph, try closing your eyes, focusing on your breathing, and seeing what comes into your mind, completely effortlessly. Allow images, thoughts, words, feelings, to flow freely, and see what your unconscious wisdom might want to reveal to you today. Remember this exercise, do it often, so that you regularly open your channels for growth and insights. Spend perhaps ten to fifteen breaths on this exercise, as a minimum, and make *no effort*, just watch what comes to mind now.

For our final emotional healing exercise, I would like to introduce you to the basic approach for emotional release which Wilhelm Reich developed fifty years ago, and which remains as a primary means of growing through old inhibitions and buried feelings.

EMOTIONAL HEALING SESSION

Set aside half an hour or so for this exercise, and find a quiet retreat where you won't be disturbed for this period of time. If you live with others, you can honestly tell them what you are going to do, so that if perchance you vocalize some feelings, they will understand when they hear you.

First of all, to charge your body with a little extra energy, you might want to jump for a short time, or to run on the spot or dance to some music. This will accelerate and deepen your breathing, to prepare for the emotional healing session.

Now lie on your back, preferably with loose clothing or no clothing, and bend your knees so that your feet are flat on the floor, knees fairly wide apart.

Close your eyes and focus on your breathing. Don't try to manipulate your breathing, simply observe each inhalation and the following exhalation, to see directly how you are breathing, and thus to make contact with your inner feelings at the moment.

Notice where your next inhalation comes from when you exhale, and make no effort at all to begin the following inhalation. You will discover, through this simple effortless watching, that an instinctual reflex will stimulate your muscles to inhale.

This reflex is a good one to get to know again consciously. It was the reflex which made you inhale the very first breath when you were born, and it is still there to keep your breathing active, when

27

you stop controlling your breathing.

Now allow your pelvis to move slightly as you breathe, so that you contract your stomach muscles and rotate the pelvis upwards on the exhale, as shown in the illustration; and then after a moment's pause, reverse the movement and relax the pelvis, inhaling through the nose quickly and arching your lower back off the floor as you fill with air, deep down into your belly as well as in your chest.

Continue with this pelvic rocking for a few breaths, so that you feel a charging sensation in your body. Exhale through the mouth, hold after the exhalation until you are hungry for air. Then, before inhaling, consciously relax the pelvic muscles so that the pelvis and lower back begin to arch. Once you feel this beautiful relaxation in the pelvis, allow the inhalation to come strongly through the nose, as if you are being effortlessly blown full of air.

You can vocalize a soft sighing sound as you exhale, or even make deeper pushing sounds as you totally empty your lungs of air on the exhale. Then, after perhaps six to ten breath cycles, you can relax and just breathe naturally.

Now, imagine that you are running away from something which you don't like, or are running towards something or someone that you really like. Start pounding the feet on the floor as if you are running, now, with your arms pounding the floor on either side of you also, simulating running. Allow your head to roll from side to side as in running also. Breathe through the mouth, and make whatever sounds you want.

Then stop, relax, observe your increased breathing, and continue breathing through the mouth.

We now come to the heart of the exercise. Wilhelm Reich, one of the great geniuses of modern psychology, discovered that if his clients were simply allowed to lie and breathe deeply through the mouth for a period of a few minutes, emotions would often spontaneously start to move up and out of the body. This natural

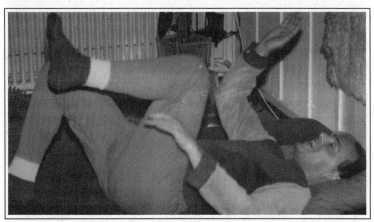

flow of emotions would generate a discharge that was, in itself, very healing, allowing old pains and emotional wounds to be released, and a new sense of vitality to enter the body.

So you can tap this natural healing process yourself, by simply breathing deeply through the mouth, allowing whatever sounds that want to come out to be vocalized, and making whatever movements of your body that come naturally. You might find yourself feeling like crying, for instance. Allow these feelings to express themselves. You might also feel anger, which you can release through vocalization and pounding on the floor.

What is important is that you surrender to whatever feelings might arise. At first you might feel frightened, or embarrassed, at sudden unexpected emotions which rise to the surface, but breathe into these feelings, allow them their time for expression. You will feel much better afterwards, and will have learned something new about your deeper emotions.

It is vital that you remain aware of your breathing throughout this exercise. The breath awareness is your vehicle into your hidden emotions — this is why we are so often totally unaware of our breathing, because we want to avoid certain feelings. But I encourage you to reverse this denial pattern of blocked emotions. Consciously allow whatever emotions are under pressure inside you to come up and be gone.

This exercise is also preparation for when you find someone to share your deeper feelings with. If you can do this basic exercise when you are with another person, you will be able to express your feelings more honestly, to let the emotions flow, so that your friend can get to know you better. And in order to be able to do this with another person, you should first learn to do it with yourself!

My recommendation is that you do this basic breathing/emotional healing exercise once a day in its full form, and also do it in a modified manner many times a day: perhaps once an hour, no matter what you are doing, pause for just six breaths, turn your total awareness to the air rushing in and out your nose and mouth, and just watch to see what you are feeling at the moment.

When you are interacting with other people, do this exercise: see if you can remain aware of your breathing, and thus of your feelings, as you talk. Stay in touch with your whole body at once, so that you interact not only with your head and your thoughts, but with your whole body. This is the state you will want to maintain when you meet someone you really like — so you need to practise until it is a new habit.

You will find, when you maintain your awareness of your breathing while you are talking with someone, that the quality of your conversations deepens. When you consciously connect your thinking and talking with your heart and breathing, even with your power centre down deeper in your belly and pelvis, you activate an intuitive flow of thoughts and words which taps the vast reservoir of your wisdom. Practise this, and see how it changes your relating with people in general.

REVIEW OF PART TWO

First we asked the seven basic questions about your childhood. These are questions to consider a number of times.

Then we looked at eight primary needs, to see how well your mother and father satisfied these needs, and we compared your present needs with those which you had as a child.

We then offered several therapy games you can play with yourself, to help with emotional clarity and healing.

We evaluated your present emotional feelings, asked six special questions, and then, as the primary healing exercise, learned the 'emotional healing session'.

PART THREE

Preparing Yourself for a New Relationship

In the last section, we considered ways in which you can begin to heal old emotional wounds, and to grow beyond the inhibitions which block honest, successful relating with people. In this new chapter, we are going to look at positive ways in which you can actively expand your personality, enhance your personal power and attraction, and consciously develop qualities which are universally considered desirable by the people around you.

There has been much talk, during the last three decades, about personality growth. Many psychological schools have been developed which can aid in our personality growth, and this chapter certainly draws from that tradition; but I would like to take this opportunity to go a step deeper than most of the formal psychological techniques do. During the last dozen years, my colleagues and I have been exploring particular techniques and meditations which seem to greatly accelerate the process of personality growth. These techniques are in no way dangerous, and you should be readily able to apply them to your own life, and to benefit from them.

Rather than focusing on particular aspects of your personality, we are going to focus on your primary awareness of yourself as a whole. Awareness is, of course, the key to an expanding, evolving personality. To the extent that we are aware of our deeper selves, we radiate a more vital presence, and it is this vital presence which is most attractive to the outside world.

So our first focus will be on the direct expansion of your awareness of yourself, and of the outside world. This is not esoteric work, by the way, it is a simple expansion of your perceptual abilities. As such, it almost always brings a feeling of more power, relaxation, and pleasure into the body. We tend to live mostly in our heads, with little contact with our whole bodies. This next exercise will begin the integration of your thinking with the rest of your being. Naturally, some of you will have already learned these meditations on your own, but my experience is that most of us, including myself, can benefit from the regular habit of the following meditation.

PERSONAL PRESENCE EXERCISE

Stand quietly where you won't be disturbed for five minutes, and close your eyes.

Begin with a simple awareness of your feet on the ground. Then expand that awareness to include the movements of your breathing as you breathe without effort. Do this for perhaps six breaths, holding your focus of attention to your feet and your breathing at the same time.

Now, while remaining aware of your breathing, especially of the air going in and out of your nose, expand that awareness to include your whole body at once.

At first, you will perhaps find this impossible to do, or confusing. We tend to be aware of particular parts of our bodies at a time, rather than the whole body at once. But if you do this exercise ten or twelve times, simply giving yourself the verbal suggestion to 'be aware of your whole body at once', you will find that, each time you say this to yourself, or listen to it on one of the available cassette tapes, a new experience comes to you! Suddenly, at some point in time, you will experience a definite sensation of 'being aware of your whole body at once'.

There are millions of nerve endings in all parts of the body, which constantly monitor the position of your body in space, and send this information to a particular centre in your brain. When I ask you to be aware of your left knee right now, for instance, you will find that your awareness can focus on this inner sensation.

'Being aware of your whole body at once' means expanding this body awareness to the entire region of the brain which processes the body-position information. In the same way that we can either

focus our seeing on a point, or just look to see everything at once (an exercise we will do soon), we can also turn our inner attention to a complete awareness, rather than the normal focusing on a point.

Curiously, you can't make yourself expand your consciousness. You can give yourself a verbal suggestion, and simply observe what happens in your consciousness — but you cannot force an expansion. It is effortless. When we exert any kind of pressure or force, we do this through a contraction. We tense our bodies to push something, for instance. But with the expansion of our awareness, we must simply allow the natural expansion to occur.

Developing this ability to expand one's awareness to include the breathing and the whole body at once has become the beginning point with

all clients in my therapy practice. When this basic awareness has been tapped, all other
aspects of emotional growth
can occur much faster, and at
deeper levels.

And when it comes to finding each other, this expanded
state of awareness is vital in
helping you attain your desired goal. When you expand
your consciousness from just
thoughts and ideas to include your whole being at once, the world
around you appears quite different, and new possibilities begin to
develop.

Also, in this state, which is continually changing and never the
same twice, everything feels new to you. You feel vital, fresh, very
much alive in the present moment, and in this state, you will
naturally find that people are more attracted to you. You have
something which most people lack — a sense of self-awareness, a
responsiveness to the present moment.

So once again, let's begin to develop this ability, so that it
becomes a new, positive habit, replacing old habits of constricted
awareness: say to yourself, "I am aware of my breathing now. I can
feel the movement as I breathe in my body. And now, I am expanding my awareness to include both my breathing, and my whole
body at once."

You can do this with eyes closed, or open, but in the beginning,
it is easiest to do it with your eyes closed. Remember that practising
this simple exercise, which takes less than a minute to do, is the key
to expanding success.

SPACE AWARENESS

The third step in this consciousness expansion exercise is a natural
development from the first two, but all too often completely

forgotten. After you have become aware of your breathing, and then also your body, you can expand your awareness to include a feeling for the space around you, for the actual air which is in the room right now.

With your eyes closed, you can sense the space around you, especially as you breathe the air in from the outside world. At this point, when you are aware of your breathing, and your body, and the air around you, you are in a state of total awareness.

If you remember the 'lucky' person we were talking about earlier, who seemed to have a magic charm for attracting people, you might begin at this point to realize what one of that person's natural qualities was: this very state of mind we have been moving into!

What we have found in the last decade of research into the nature of encounter, is that people in this expanded state of awareness, who are in touch with their breathing, their whole body at once, and the space around them at the same time, are in fact the people who can actively move through the world and find the right people to relate with.

Obviously, a person who is fully present in her or his body will be most responsive emotionally as well as intellectually, with a vitality and a presence which is much desired.

SEEING WITH YOUR WHOLE BODY

Especially when we find ourselves looking at someone who attracts us, we tend to become so engrossed in the outside world, that we lose our intimate contact with our own body. This directly hinders our relating abilities, because we lose touch with our own emotional responses to the other person.

So as the next step in this personality-expansion exercise, we should develop the ability to open our eyes and at the same time remain aware of our breathing and our whole body at once, as we have been doing in the last pages. This might seem like a simple challenge, but try it, and see what your habits are:

Stand or sit with your eyes closed, and focus on your breathing.

Now expand your awareness to include your whole body at once.

Expand your awareness one step further to include the space around you, the air you are breathing.

Now allow your eyes to open slowly. Simply notice what happens to your awareness of your breathing, and your body, when your eyes open.

Also, notice if your eyes immediately look for a particular object to focus on, or if they gaze at the entire visual field at once.

If you discovered that you tend to lose your awareness of your breathing and your body when you open your eyes, let me suggest a key for remaining aware of yourself when you are looking out at the world.

SEEING EVERYTHING AT ONCE

The Papago Indians have a special technique of seeing, familiar throughout the American Southwest Indians, in which they look to see everything at once, instead of looking to focus on a point. Our tradition strongly conditions us always to have our eyes focused at some point in space. We have a strong 'fixation' habit, but there is a completely different way of using the eyes.

With your eyes open, look in order to see the space around you, not to see the objects. To do this, simply stare in front of you, but let your eyes go just slightly out of focus. Bring your awareness back to your breathing if it has been lost, and maintain most of your awareness not on your visual experience, but on the experience of your body. When you do this properly, it will seem as if you are looking at yourself, and at the same time seeing the entire visual world at once.

This is similar to the za-zen visual techniques of the Buddhist traditions also, and is a general means of expanding one's consciousness. Our visual habits tend to reflect our deeper awareness habits as well. When you always focus on a point visually, you tend always to focus on a point when you look inward also. And what we are working towards here is the opposite. Certainly, focusing on a point is of value, and much of our visual work depends on such seeing. But we need the opposite end of the spectrum included also if we are going to integrate our seeing with our internal awareness.

This perception trick is also central in the martial arts traditions of the Orient, where the karate or judo master remains aware of everything in the perceptual field, and is instantly ready to react to whatever he sees.

The beauty of this type of perception is that, when you are 'seeing everything at once', or 'seeing with the body 'as the Indians call it, your thinking becomes silent. You find yourself totally in the present moment, and in this condition you are in the optimum state for responding spontaneously to the outside world — and if this outside world is someone you want to respond to, then your relating will be optimal.

For instance, when we look at someone, we tend to fixate on first one eye, then the other, then the mouth, etc. But you can also see 'everything at once' by using the above exercise. You can see the whole face or even a person's complete body at once, and you will find that your bodily response to this person is enhanced with this form of seeing.

So practise this way of seeing everything at once regularly, many times a day, and allow it to become a habit in your seeing, so that when you want to you can instantly, and effortlessly, shift to seeing with your body.

DEVELOPING PERSONAL POWER

The exercise you just learned is actually the first exercise in a twelve-step programme which my colleagues and I have developed for enhancing a person's sense of personal power and presence. At this point, I would like to teach you that full programme. The trick of this programme, which separates it from other movement/vitality programmes, is that you maintain the heightened state of awareness developed in the first exercise, while you move through the following exercises. In this way you tap very deep reservoirs of energy, and with each exercise you will find your awareness expanding in a particular direction, so that at the end of the twelve exercises, you are in a tremendously vital state.

My recommendation is that you do these twelve exercises every morning, so that you fully wake yourself up, tap into your vital energies, and go into each new day in this expanded state of vitality. You can do a quick version of the exercises in only four to five minutes, or you can take more time and spend ten or fifteen minutes expanding your personal power. There are cassette tapes which will guide you through the exercises if you wish, also.

So set aside some time for yourself, and begin by standing quietly, your eyes closed. Don't make any effort to change how you feel right now, just turn your attention inward and see what you find.

Exercise One

Centring

> Stand quietly, your eyes closed. Turn your attention gently to your breathing. Feel the air as it rushes in and out through your nose. Be aware of the movements in your body as you breathe.
>
> Expand your awareness to include also your whole body at once, from your feet to the top of your head. Allow your body

to straighten slightly as you inhale, and your pelvis to rotate forward slightly as you exhale.

Allow your awareness to expand again, to include the space around you, the air that you are breathing. Stay aware of your breathing and your body as you feel the space of the room around you.

When your eyes want to, allow them to open effortlessly.

Look down at the floor, and make no effort to see anything. Instead, remain focused inward on your breathing and your body, and simply see everything at once.

Exercise Two

Rolling

Close your eyes again, and begin to do neck rolls, making slow, gentle circles with your head as you remain aware of your breathing and your whole body at once. Inhale through the nose as your head moves up in the circle, and exhale through the mouth as it moves downwards in the circle.

 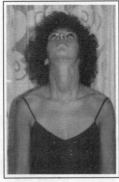 

Make a sighing sound, with your jaw relaxed and open, as you exhale. When you are ready, allow your eyes to open as you continue to make circles. Reverse the direction of the circles every two or three breaths.

Exercise Three

Shaking

Now that you have loosened up your neck, and allowed your breathing to expand somewhat, you can quickly awaken your whole body: first, shake your head back and forth. Do this slowly at first, with your eyes open and your jaw relaxed. Make a slight 'aahhh' sound. Then do it more quickly, with your tongue out. Let any feelings inside you begin to discharge. Now shake your hands, raising them above your head and down again, while continuing to vocalize. At the same time, lift a leg

and shake your foot and knee. Then shift and shake the other leg. Finally, shake your whole body, as if you are dancing to a crazy jazz tune.

For the final shaking sequence, we are going to do a kicking movement to open fully your pelvic area. Stand on one foot, and start swinging the other leg forward and backwards, in a gentle kicking motion. Exhale as you kick forward, and inhale as your leg swings back.

Let your arms move naturally, as if you are walking, and slap the bottom of your kicking foot on the ground as it comes back each time. Enjoy this movement, and allow your pelvis and torso to move also. Do this three or four times, and then switch feet.

Exercise Four

Jumping

To complete the awakening section of this programme, start jumping gently, just barely bringing your feet off the ground. Let your heels touch when you land. Breathe through the mouth, inhaling for two jumps, and exhaling for two jumps. Make sure your shoulders are loose, and your breathing expansive. Jump until you are ready to stop, and never push yourself to jump more than ten times.

Pause a moment after these first four exercises, close your eyes, and become aware of your breathing, your body, and the space around you at once. Just notice how your feelings in your body have changed through these four exercises. Accept whatever emotions might be present when you look inward. You can discharge them in the coming exercises.

Exercise Five

Massaging

Close your eyes if they are open, and massage your face with your hands. Don't think of any technique, just touch your hands to your face and see what your fingers want to do today. Sigh with an open mouth and relaxed jaw, and make whatever sounds you want to.

At this point, or even sooner in the programme, you might find yourself wanting to yawn and stretch spontaneously. Always surrender to this urge fully! Yawning and stretching are your body's natural means of revitalization.

Exercise Six

Hanging

Stand with your feet wide apart, your eyes closed, and slowly, with knees slightly bent, bend over forwards. Exhale deeply through the mouth, and go down until you touch the ground. Slap the floor vigorously a few times, and shake your head to make sure it is relaxed and loose.

You can discharge any emotional pressure vigorously in this position by opening your mouth, sticking your tongue out like a little child, and making whatever sound come spontaneously. Notice how your breathing deepens.

Then slowly, very slowly, start coming up, with your head down until last. Stand with eyes closed and be aware of your breathing, your body, the space around you.

Exercise Seven

Pounding

With your eyes still closed, start pounding with the inside of your fist as shown in the illustration, on your head and neck. Gently but vigorously pound all over your head, while making soft 'aaahhh' sounds through the mouth.

Pound also on your neck, and then on your chest, making Tarzan sounds. Then pound strongly on your stomach and abdomen regions, continuing with the 'aaahhh!' sounds.

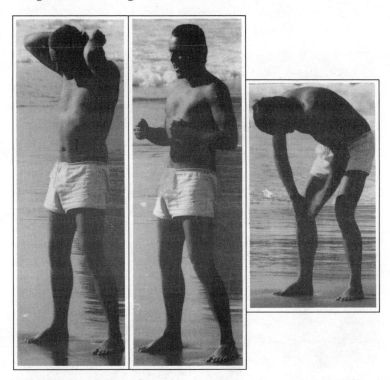

Now slap your legs with an open hand, all the way down to your feet and back up, and finish with a good slapping on your lower back region.

Exercise Eight

Hitting

Stand with feet fairly wide apart, facing a mirror if you have one. Then make a good fist with both hands, and start hitting an invisible target in front of you, first with one fist, then with the other, as shown in the illustration.

With every hit, make a solid' POW!' sound. Begin very gently and playfully with this exercise, and then build up in speed and sounds until you feel your power flowing.

However, never lose your feeling of playfulness with this exercise. You want to develop your ability to feel your power, while also feeling the enjoyment of your power. Bringing the two together is the key.

You can also raise both fists into the air, as shown in the illustration, and hit downwards onto an imaginary table in front of you. Make a 'Haaiiiii ya!' sound as you do so, charging your body with energy with the hands over the head, and then releasing the energy as you hit downwards with the 'ya!' part of the sound.

Once again, do this exercise playfully, feeling your power, but not

scaring yourself with it. And make sure that you keep your fists tight and powerful.

After this eighth exercise, pause again, close your eyes, watch your breathing, your whole body at once, and be aware of the space around you for a moment.

Exercise Nine

Stretching

This next exercise is called 'the fencer's stretch'. Stand with feet at right angles to each other, as shown in the illustration. Lock your hands together behind you, and slowly, bending *both* knees equally, bend down towards the toe of your left foot.

Bend down until your head is near your knee, and look at the tip of your foot throughout the exercise. Exhale down, with the mouth wide as if to bite! Make a powerful but controlled 'Haaaaaa!' sound as you bend down towards your toe, until you are totally empty of air.

While still looking at your toe, inhale as you slowly and powerfully stand upright, filling your chest with air. But keep looking at your toe.

Repeat this movement three times, for three breaths, noticing how each movement expands your breathing and your feeling of power. Then do the same movement over your right toe for three breath cycles.

Exercise Ten

Pleasure rocking

Lie down on your back with your knees bent and your feet flat on the ground, knees apart. First just watch your breathing. Make no effort to inhale after your next exhalation. Simply watch how your body naturally generates a new inhalation, after you hold your breath a few moments. This breath reflex is your best friend!

Now slowly start contracting your abdominal muscles as you exhale, pressing your lower back against the floor and rotating your pelvis upwards. Exhale through the mouth, making a sighing sound.

Hold your breath after the exhalation until you feel hungry for air. Then, before inhaling, relax your muscles and let your pelvis relax onto the floor.

At this point, allow the air to rush into your lungs, through the nose, quickly and powerfully. Arch your lower back off the ground, and allow your pelvis to rotate backwards and down. There should be a feeling of pleasure in this movement on the inhalation.

Then with the exhalation, open your mouth and sigh as you powerfully and slowly push the air totally out of your lungs. Hold a moment in this state of contraction. Then relax the pelvis again, and finally allow the air to rush into your lungs on the next inhalation through the nose.

Continue with this pelvic rocking, until you want to stop. Surrender to the pleasure which comes from the movement.

Exercise Eleven

Charging

Roll over onto your stomach now, and just watch your breathing, and expand your awareness to your whole body.

This next exercise is drawn from the Guatemalan Indian tradition, and is a very powerful meditation for gaining a sense of increased energy and vitality in the body. Place your hand over your forehead as shown in the illustration, and place your other hand over that hand.

Lower your head down, with your elbows out comfortably to each side. Breathe effortlessly. Imagine that you are looking down directly to the centre of the earth. With your eyes closed, you can actually feel gravity pulling your eyes directly towards the centre of the earth. Feel this alignment, but make no mental effort.

Exercise Twelve

Manifesting

Come up onto your hands and knees like a cat. As you inhale, arch your back down and raise your head upwards as shown in the illustration. Inhale through the nose. You will notice that your breathing and your pelvic movements are the same for this exercise as for the pleasure rocking exercise.

As you exhale through the mouth, growl like a cat and reverse your pelvic position, arching your back up as you push all the air strongly and slowly out of your lungs until you are looking down and back between your legs.

As you continue with this cat stretching, feel your own power in your body, and enjoy that feeling, growling with a sense of satisfaction in your power. Feel the direct relationship between the movement of power, and of pleasure. This is an essential relationship to discover!

THE PERSONAL POWER PROGRAMME AT A GLANCE

Once you learn this programme by heart, you can move through the exercises as rapidly or slowly as you want. But first, you will want to do the movements enough times so that your body 'knows' them and you no longer have to think about which one comes next.

Exercise One	Centring
Exercise Two	Rolling
Exercise Three	Shaking
Exercise Four	Jumping
Exercise Five	Massaging
Exercise Six	Hanging
Exercise Seven	Pounding
Exercise Eight	Hitting
Exercise Nine	Stretching
Exercise Ten	Pleasure rocking
Exercise Eleven	Charging
Exercise Twelve	Manifesting

Because these movements stimulate many instinctive feelings, and activate spontaneous breathing patterns that are often inhibited, the movements in themselves are a therapy programme. And you will find, after doing the twelve exercises, that your consciousness has been expanded beautifully.

FROM ANXIETY TO PERSONAL POWER

Anxiety is certainly the primary emotion which blocks our reaching out for companionship. In the last chapter, we explored some of the ways in which we can begin to overcome anxiety so that we have more confidence in acting to satisfy our interpersonal needs. In this present discussion, I want to expand upon our understanding of anxiety, especially with regards to your sense of personal power and confidence.

Anxiety and personal power are actually opposite poles of one continuum. When you are totally filled with anxiety, you have no personal power at all, and conversely, when you feel full of your personal power, you feel no anxiety at all. When I first began my career as a therapist, I worked very hard to help people reduce their fears and anxieties, but I had little success with traditional techniques. It was only when I returned to my childhood experiences with the Indian community I grew up in, that I re-discovered an approach to anxiety which worked.

This approach did not bother with a person's anxiety at all. Instead of focusing upon fears and inhibitions, I focused upon the opposite. I focused on how to help a person increase his or her sense of personal power; when this sense of inner strength and self-assurance increased, the anxiety levels decreased equally, by themselves.

At the same time that I began applying American Indian rituals to therapy situations, I became exposed to the teachings and therapy techniques of Wilhelm Reich, the third great European pioneer in psychology following Freud and Jung. I was amazed to find that Reich's understanding of personal power was almost identical with the American Indian understanding. So in presenting this programme on how to increase your feeling of personal power, I wish to thank both traditions for their insights and actual techniques.

How do you feel about your own personal power? Do you have a feeling of inner strength and confidence, or do you feel somewhat shaky deep-down inside you? Be as honest as you can at this point, so you can begin to grow right from where you really find yourself, right now. All of us suffer from anxiety from time to time, and all of us have our weak points. What is important is your willingness to face your weak points, and to learn ways of expanding your sense of personal power so that your weak points no longer detract from your ability to go out and actively explore the world around you.

In both the Indian and the Reichian traditions, a person's breathing is the barometer of personal power or anxiety, so we will once again turn to look at your breathing. Consider the following questions, to see which statements apply to you. We are not trying to categorize you through these statements, but simply to begin your looking directly at your own breathing patterns, and the accompanying strengths or weaknesses:

YOUR PERSONAL POWER INVENTORY

1. Is your breathing usually shallow, tight, and high in the chest?   Yes ___ No ___

2. Can you exhale deeply, with a feeling of power down in the abdominal region?   Yes ___ No ___

3. Are you mostly aware of your inhalations, wanting to be full of air rather than empty?   Yes ___ No ___

4. Do you catch yourself holding your breath a lot during the day?   Yes ___ No ___

5. Do you enjoy running, playing vigorously, to the point at which your breathing is powerful and your heart-beat powerful also?   Yes___ No___

6. When you are in a challenging, perhaps frightening situation, does your breathing freeze, and your ability to act freeze also?   Yes ___ No___

7. Are you aware of your breathing most of the time, noticing how it changes in different emotional situations?   Yes___ No ___

8. When you are in intimate situations, does your breathing become shallow, tight, inhibited?   Yes___ No___

Personal power is not necessarily your physical strength alone. We all know big strong men who are quite weak when it comes to emotional situations, for instance; and many women who are physically inferior can be extremely powerful in their expression of their demands. What really determines personal power is your ability to mobilize your strength when it is needed, either emotionally, mentally, or physically.

This is where your breathing determines all. When you are inhaling, you do not have much power. When you are exhaling, your power is available to you. For instance, if you are going to push a car, you exhale strongly, rather than inhaling as you push.

In fact, we have found that people feel anxiety when they are focused on their inhaling, and they feel personal power when they are focused on their exhaling. When the exhalation is deep and strong, one feels almost no anxiety. Only when the breathing becomes inhibited, frozen with fear, tight and shallow, does anxiety grip us. In the final analysis, anxiety *is* this breathing pattern. You cannot separate them.

So if you want to be free of your anxieties when it comes to relating with people, you will want to follow these basic breathing rules:

Rule one If you want to reduce anxiety, focus on your exhalations, and make them as deep and smooth as possible.

Rule two If you want to increase your sense of personal power at a particular time, make your exhalations slow, and push the air out completely with a contraction of your abdomen.

Rule three When you feel yourself becoming weak and anxious in a social situation, immediately bring your focus to your breathing, as in the first exercise in the Personal Power Programme. Forget the outside world for a moment, and regain your inner centre.

Rule four If you notice yourself becoming anxious in the presence of other people, relax your jaw muscles and exhale slowly and powerfully through the mouth. This can be done without anyone noticing, and it will bring you back in touch with your personal power.

Curiously, every time you become anxious, you will find that the first step to anxiety is always a thought. We should look at the process which generates anxiety in your body a moment, so that you can begin to see your own habits, and in seeing them, begin to reverse them.

We can only feel fear when we feel threatened. Fear is a reaction to a danger we perceive. If we see a dog that is dangerous, our mind takes in the visual stimulus, analyses it, and then comes the thought: this dog could hurt me!

It is this thought which then stimulates the fear response, as the mind sends out messages throughout the body to prepare the body to fight, or to run away.

When your mind sees a real danger, it is to your advantage to become frightened, for the fear charges your body with energy, and you can then use this energy to attack, or to run away.

The problem comes, especially in relating with people, when your mind has a bad habit of seeing 'danger' when there really is no danger. You were perhaps frightened of some social situation when you were a child, and now, every time you are in a similar situation, automatically your mind thinks 'danger' and begins the physical reaction which you feel as anxiety.

What can you do about this reaction?

First of all, become aware of how your breathing is affected when the anxiety reaction takes place. Your breathing will become tight, shallow, often frozen altogether. This inhibition of the breathing will obviously reduce your oxygen intake, thus reducing your physical strength, and making your mind dizzy.

Luckily, we can consciously control our breathing, when we are aware of it. If you have an unconscious habit of freezing your breathing in particular social situations, you can alter this habit when you become conscious of it, and take direct control of your breathing. You can follow the four rules above, and directly reduce your anxiety as you breathe in the pattern of personal power.

Notice once again, that the key is your increased awareness of yourself! You must realize what you do as a habit, in order to begin to change that habit.

Let me give you a couple of final insights into the relationship of breathing and personal power:

When you are full of air, you are weak and in danger of an anxiety attack.

When you are almost empty of air and pushing with the abdominal muscles to empty yourself slowly of air, you are in a position of maximum personal power.

A slow, abdominal exhalation, with the jaw relaxed and the mind aware of the whole body at once, gives you maximum strength and confidence.

Anxiety reduces your awareness of your breathing and your body, as well as collapsing your awareness of the space around you. The more you develop the opposite ability, of expanding

your awareness as we have learned to, the more you enhance
your sense of personal power.

BECOMING MORE ATTRACTIVE

Do you consider yourself attractive to other people, especially to
the particular sort of people you would like to begin a relationship
with?

To end this chapter, we should focus on your self-image and
begin to improve it where needed. All too often, people carry
around in their heads a negative self-image, which continually
inhibits their growth and success in relating with others.

What about you?

Do you like the way you look?

Do you think other people like the way you appear to them?

Do you feel you are sexually appealing?

Can people see that deep-down, you are ugly and not really
worth relating with?

Do you think you are worth relating with?

I was once a therapist in Los Angeles, working with very
beautiful women in the entertainment industry, and I was regularly amazed at how ugly these women sometimes felt. And
conversely, some very homely, physically unattractive people are
often very sexually enticing, because their inner vitality is bloom-
ing with love and energy.

So your ability to attract someone to you is not a matter of your
genetic inheritance. It is a matter of the inner fire that burns
brightly, or is inhibited.

Once again, if you need to brighten your inner fire, you must begin not in pushing yourself into external situations, but rather, turn inward and focus on the fire itself. If you feel ugly, you are ugly. If you feel beautiful, the right people will find you beautiful also.

The keys to general attractiveness have already been given in our discussion so far:

1. You need to release the negative feelings inside you, if you want to stop projecting these negative feelings in your social relating.

2. You need to increase your inner awareness, so that you are present in your body, in order for your body to appear attractive.

3. Frozen breathing, and frozen movement, leads to a reduction in attractiveness. Expanding your breathing, and increasing your movement habits, will make you more vital and attractive.

4. Caring for yourself and loving yourself are the first steps in finding others to love you and care for you.

You will notice that I have avoided completely the usual self-improvement techniques of 'positive thinking'. I have not encouraged you to block out your negative feelings, and to force a positive self-image on yourself. I find this ultimately futile, and quite unfair to your deeper self.

Instead, the focus is on directly looking to see your whole self, accepting yourself as you are right now, and following certain meditations and exercises which can help you expand into a more vital, attractive person.

Right now, we should reflect before moving on to the next chapter, and see what your image of yourself is — do you love yourself?

If you do not love yourself, if you have a negative feeling towards yourself, it is going to be very difficult for someone to love you. Your negative self-image is going to be projected in everything you say, every move of your body. So before seeking out a friend in the outside world, it is necessary to become your own best friend first.

BECOMING YOUR OWN BEST FRIEND

It is a basic rule in psychology, and in the realms of common sense and experience as well, that you cannot love another person unless you first love yourself. Jesus encouraged us to 'love our neighbour as we love ourselves', and if we do not love ourselves, we are not going to love our neighbour either.

The first step in expanding your love for yourself is to be totally honest about how you feel towards yourself now. If you dislike yourself, you do yourself no good by pretending to like yourself.

To find out how you feel towards yourself, you can look either to your thoughts, to your mental impressions of yourself, or to your feelings, to your actual emotional relationship with yourself.

First of all, spend some time thinking about how you feel towards yourself. You can use the following list of statements to evaluate your self-image:

SELF-IMAGE EVALUATION

(a) "Usually, I like the way I look."   (Yes or no.)

(b) "I feel good inside, most of the time."   (Yes or no.)

(c) "When I wake up in the morning, I am
    happy to find myself looking back at me
    in the mirror."   (Yes or no.)

(d) "I usually do the best I can in situations, and
    I don't feel guilty for how I lead my life."   (Yes or no.)

(e) "I might not be perfect, but I am definitely
just fine the way I am."   (Yes or no.)

(f) "I can accept myself as I am."   (Yes or no.)

(g) "Sure, I love myself!"   (Yes or no.)

(h) "I consider myself my own best friend." (True or false.)

As with earlier questions, the aim of this list is not to judge yourself, but simply to look and see the reality of your feelings towards yourself. Most of your negative self-images are old habits, mostly unconscious. We want to bring them to the surface so that you can get a good look at them, and see if they are valid or not.

As long as you feel there is something wrong with you, you put up a barrier that keeps other people from accepting you. If you don't accept yourself, no one else can either. It's that simple.

All too often, we were brought up by parents and teachers who tried to mould us into a particular personality which just didn't fit us. We were told to be different from the person we naturally were. So we tried to change how we were, but deep-down, we knew that we were simply our natural selves; and if our natural selves didn't match the image our parents and teachers wanted us to fit, then we felt somehow inadequate, unacceptable, unlikeable.

At this point in your life, you can throw off all that old conditioning. You can finally say to the world. "Hey, I might not be perfect, I might not be exactly what you want me to be, but I am okay just as I am!"

Can you say this to the world? Or are you afraid of being rejected if people find out who you really are? Do you hide behind an image, or do you let people see you directly? Can you even see yourself directly, or are you lost in your image of your ideal self?

You can't try to change yourself at this point. You can only look and see what your mental habits are, and in the act of looking honestly, you will generate a natural change deep within you. Really look at yourself. Breathe into what you find. Accept how you are. And you will find that you suddenly start to grow, to change, to become more yourself.

In the final analysis, if you are going to establish a satisfying relationship, you are going to have to let this person see you for who you are. And if you are hiding your deeper self from the world because you think it is ugly or unacceptable, you are not giving anyone the chance to love you as you are.

What would happen in your life if you stopped trying to make yourself better, if you stopped trying to impress people with how great you are, and simply let the world relate to you as you naturally are? This is a vital question, and one you must risk finding the answer to, before you can really establish satisfying relationships.

You can see how this will work in the opposite direction as well — if you are hard on yourself, judging yourself harshly, not accepting your weak points, you are going to judge others that way also, and reject them because they are less than perfect. This will double your difficulty in finding someone to relate deeply with. Real love is simple acceptance. If you love someone for who they could become, instead of for who they are in the present, you are not really loving them. It works the same in your love for yourself.

A good friend accepts you as you are, and gives you space to grow into your natural self. If you are going to be your own best friend, you must feel the same way towards yourself.

Interestingly, if you don't accept yourself as you are, there is no hope for you ever becoming anything better. Real personality growth is always a fulfilment of your natural potential. If you feel your basic self is unacceptable, that self will never be able to expand into its full expression. You can only become more completely who you are right now. So who you are right now must be OK. Insist on the world treating you in this way, and you will become lovable!

EVALUATION OF PROGRESS SO FAR

We can now look back and reflect upon insights gained in the first three sections:

<u>First</u> How do you feel about your mental clarity regarding your interpersonal needs?

<u>Second</u>   Reflect upon your emotional readiness for beginning a new relationship.

<u>Third</u> Have you developed a growing awareness of your own body, your own presence, your own inner centre?

<u>Fourth</u> Are you on the path to expanding your sense of personal power?

<u>Fifth</u>   Are you exploring your potential for increasing your inner vitality, and your external attractiveness?

<u>Sixth</u>   Do you feel ready to let someone come into your life, without losing your own centre in the process?

<u>Seventh</u>   Are you now ready to begin the process of actively attracting the desired person to you, and of going out into the world to meet this person?

PART FOUR
Attracting the Right Person

The premise of this section, and in fact of this entire book and programme, is that there is someone out there in the world, right at this very moment, who is wanting to meet you just as much as you are wanting to meet him or her.

There are millions of people who feel similar unfulfilled needs to yours, and in spite of your particular personality idiosyncrasies, there are certainly many people with whom you can form mutually fulfilling relationships. The question is, at this point, how do you meet them, and what habits are you maintaining which limit your potential for meeting them?

In this chapter we are going to consider the final four factors that encourage, or block, your encounter with a new person:

First of all, there is the matter of timing. Are you usually lost in thoughts of the future, or memories of the past, or are you living in the here and now where your new encounter will occur?

Secondly, do you have perceptual habits which keep you from directly looking to see who is around you, habits which limit your visual contact with the outside world?

Third, do you have movement patterns which keep you from coming into contact with people in general, and which need to be expanded so that you have more contacts?

Finally, we come to the actual attraction meditations which can powerfully enhance your potential for encounter.

What happens though, if you arrive finally at that awaited moment, encounter someone you really want, and find that your habit of always living for the future blocks you from now being in the present moment?

This is a very serious problem. We actually lose our ability simply to exist in the present moment. We are so conditioned to living for the future, we don't know how to live in the present.

When doing workshops, I often ask the group simply to watch their breathing for five minutes, remain completely in the present moment, without going off into thoughts of the past or the future. Almost without exception, no one can stay in the present moment for five minutes. Most of them cannot remain in the present for even one moment. Simple awareness of the movement of time, of the eternal present, has been lost completely.

So when you do meet the right person, what happens? You will be so much in the future, lost in thought, that you might not be able simply to relate in the present moment satisfactorily. The mental habit can be so strong that it dominates you even when it is no longer necessary.

In order to avoid a breakdown of your encounter when it happens, we can begin to alter this future-projection habit of your mind right now, if it is a problem. Let's do a simple test and see your present past/present/future condition.

LIVING IN THE PRESENT MOMENT

When we are thinking, we are not really in the present moment. Thought requires concepts, and concepts are completely generated from past experience. We can think *about* the present moment, but our thinking always takes us into the past. Thought is reflection, not the actual experiential present. Thinking is certainly a worthwhile activity at times. But to be a prisoner of thought, unable to turn it off so as to experience directly the present moment, is detrimental to human relating. People who are always in their heads are not available for emotional contact.

What about you?

In a moment, after reading these instructions, I would like you to close this book, and turn your awareness only to what is actually happening in the present moment, both inside you, and around you. You can be aware of what you hear, what you see, what you smell, and what you feel. You can be aware of your breathing, your body and the air around you.

See how long you can go without a thought coming up, and pulling you away from the present experience of the moment. Don't judge yourself, don't force yourself to remain in the present moment. Simply begin to see your habits in terms of thought/experience. So close the book now, and see what happens, how many breaths you can count before you lose the present.

How did you do?

One of the great contemporary spiritual teachers whom I had the good fortune to study under, Krishnamurti, taught a simple exercise for helping us remain in the present moment. In fact, I just suggested it to you in the last exercise, and will clarify it now.

> To keep yourself in the present moment, you can talk to yourself in the following fashion: "Right now, I am aware of the following ... " You then tell yourself whatever sensory inputs come to your awareness, moment by moment. For instance, I will do the exercise right now, to give you an example: "I am aware of the sound of the stream running through the meadow. I am aware of my breathing, and a tension in my chest that now goes away as I watch it. I can smell the fresh air with the scent of rain and spring greenery in it. I am aware of my feet touching each other, and I now see the blue of my socks as I type these words, and now I am watching my fingers moving as I type, and I hear the stream again, and the sensation of the chair under me ... "

Try it for yourself again. Put the book down, and simply tell yourself what you are presently aware of, moment by moment. You will find this exercise immensely more easy if you first become aware of your breathing, then your whole body at once, then the air around you, and then start noting sensations.

You will find, through repeating this exercise regularly, that your ability to remain in the present moment expands step by step. You will also find that your breathing begins to relax, you find more pleasure in the present moment and you form a new habit or actually, you regain a habit from early childhood: living in the present moment and loving it!

When you do meet someone special, that person is going to exist only in this present moment. If you are not focused on the present moment, you will not even be aware of the person's presence. Only by expanding your present moment can you create space for someone new to appear in that present moment. I know this sounds very obvious, but it is one of those things we very often don't see at all, precisely because it is so obvious.

So begin right now, today. Begin allowing yourself to live in an expanded awareness of the present moment, simply watching the flow of life as it happens around you and inside you, without thought. Get to know this world well, because it is the world where you will find satisfaction of your needs. Only in the present moment are needs satisfied — this is a basic law of nature. If you are hungry, thinking about eating is not going to satisfy your actual hunger. Only at the moment you put something in your mouth does the hunger begin to be satisfied. The present moment, as the spiritual masters have been saying for thousands of years, is the only place where anything is actually happening. So we should live here, right now!

You are perhaps asking the next logical question. If the present moment is the only place where we can get satisfaction, why do most of us live in the past and the future, in our thoughts, rather than in our experiential present world?

The answer is important and simple. When we were children, before the age of five or six, we lived almost completely in the present moment, because we had not developed the conceptual abilities to project into the future, nor to dwell in the past.

Often, the present moment was not so pleasant. There was fear in the present moment, because only in the present moment did bad things happen to us. We were punished in the present moment, we got injured in the present moment, we were frightened in the present moment, and we saw things that were horrible in the present moment.

So when we developed our minds to where we could move into thought, into moving from the present into the past and the future, most of us became escape artists. We learned we could 'go away' from the present moment, we could escape from the bodily world where pain and anxiety lived, and live in a world of our own, in our fantasies, our memories, and our dreamings of the future.

We left our bodies because our bodies were the location of pain and fear. We made good our escape. We created better worlds to come in our future, and we developed the mental habit of staying in our thought worlds as much as possible, so as to avoid any possibility of a negative experience in the present moment.

In avoiding the negative, however, we also missed out on the positive, and we ended up with a mental habit which dominates us, even now.

How long did you find yourself able to remain in the present moment, without thoughts coming up and pulling you into the past or the future?

If you are constantly thinking of meeting someone in the future, you are not here working towards preparing yourself for that encounter; if you don't make steps in the present moment towards that encounter, it will never come.

So what can be done?

Simple.

Consciously develop your ability to remain in the present moment. The first exercise in Part Three, of consciousness expansion, is the primary exercise. If you can develop the habit of looking to your breathing regularly, of expanding that awareness to include your whole body at once, and then expand that awareness to take in the outside space as well, you have the key to the present moment.

And all the other exercises which we are learning, which begin with that basic awareness, are designed to strengthen your ability to live in the here-and-now.

When you meet someone new in your life, how are you going to be aware of that person? Are your thoughts going to bring you into contact with that person? Obviously not. When we are thinking, we are not really available to experience someone directly in the present moment. Only through our perceptions do we come into contact with another human being.

So we can now go one step deeper into our contact with the outside world, and discuss how our perception habits determine, and often severely limit, our ability to make contact with new people.

PERCEPTION AND RELATING POTENTIAL

I have a very close friend, whom I have known for years. She is very important to me, and satisfies many of my deeper needs. But the first three times I saw her, I didn't notice her at all. In fact, the first time I looked at her and she looked at me, I didn't even register her presence. She saw me, but I was so busy thinking about something, I completely ignored her.

Then several weeks later, the third time I actually looked at her, I suddenly was struck. I looked into her eyes, and for several moments, couldn't take my eyes away. I recognized instantly that I was looking at someone special. I didn't know in what way this person was special, but I could feel that powerful sense of recognition.

Several months later, when we had become close friends, she asked me how it had been possible for me to look right at her those first two times, and not actually see her at all. When I reflected, I remembered that I had been very much needing to meet someone like her at the time, but I was imagining the person to look different to her. I did not recognize her, nor even notice her, because she didn't fit my image of who I was looking for.

Do you have an image of the person you are looking for? Does she or he have long hair, short hair? Curly hair, or straight hair? Is this person tall or short, white-skinned or black-skinned? Is your ideal person wearing dark glasses, dressed a particular way?

These images are all from our past experiences, of course. They will never match someone in the present moment, because your past experiences will never repeat themselves. So of what value are these images you have of your ideal new friend, lover, business partner, or spiritual comrade?

Many of us go through our days looking at faces, searching for that special person, projecting our ideal image onto the faces we see, and when the faces do not match up with our ideal image, we instantly look away, rejecting the real live person because that person is not our ideal image of who we need.

This projection of an ideal image onto a person is a strong habit for most of us. Only if we become conscious of our habit can we begin to break free of it, so we can look and see the actual people around us, without judgement.

So in the days that follow, begin to observe how you do in fact look at people. And do the following exercise if you want to expand your direct perception of a new, unique human being in front of you.

You guessed it — begin with your breathing, not with the outside world. Put your awareness to yourself so that you are conscious of your body, your movements, your breathing. Then be aware of the space around you, without looking at anything in particular.

And then, in that state, allow your eyes to begin to look around you, not seeking anyone in particular, not caring what you find, just remaining centred within yourself, and seeing how you feel when you see the reality around you. If you look at a person, instantly focus on your breathing, and slowly exhale as you look, remaining aware of the physical sensations of your exhalation.

You will find that your perception is stongly altered when you look in this way. If you feel whole and complete inside your body, you will see the world as it is. Only when you feel out of touch with your own body do you see the world through your needs, your images, your ideal projections.

BREATHING THROUGH YOUR EYES

A further step in this perception exercise is to imagine that you are inhaling the world around you as you take in air, and that you are exhaling your presence and inner world into the outside world when you exhale. This gives you the proper balance in seeing. Half of the time, you are receptive to the outside world, and the other half of the time, on the exhale, you are asserting your own presence into the world.

Notice which is easier for you, to inhale and take the world in, or to exhale and send yourself out into the world. Begin this exercise right after doing the basic consciousness expansion exercise. Allow your eyes to open, looking down at the ground, not seeing anything in particular. Stay centred in your breathing, your body, and let the visual world become a part of your inner awareness.

Then you can begin to look at people while breathing and seeing together. You can take in a person as you inhale, and then send your own presence out to that person as you exhale. This is an extremely powerful exercise, which will bring you into contact with people in a unique, dynamic way.

Try it! At some point, you will find yourself looking into someone's eyes, taking them inside you as you inhale, and letting them feel your presence as you exhale — and guess who's there!

MOVEMENT AND ENCOUNTER

Even if you have successfully moved through all the previous steps in this programme, there is very little chance of your encountering the person who can fulfil your needs if you are sitting at home, hiding away somewhere, moving hardly enough to come into contact with anyone.

Take a look at yourself. First of all, did you respond positively to the movement programme in the last chapter? Did you like the idea of doing regular movement exercises, to increase your sense of vitality and personal power? Or did you, for one reason or another, reject the whole idea, preferring to remain at a low energy level, a low movement profile?

Don't judge yourself at this point, judgement is of no value, and it separates you from yourself. Just look at yourself honestly to get a clear picture of your present habits of movement.

The final section of this chapter is indeed designed to help you attract the right person to your doorstep. If you are caught in habits which avoid movement towards a desired goal, you perhaps won't even get up to answer your doorbell when your anticipated guest arrives. Most likely, for the meeting to take place, you are going to have to make some movement towards the other person too, not expecting the outside world to do all the movement for you.

We can look at movement, and lack of movement, in a very basic manner. You know you are alive, because you are moving. When you stop moving completely, you know you are dead. Movement is life. Total lack of movement is death. When we are frozen in lack-of-movement patterns and habits, we are inhibiting our lifeforce, blocking our participation in life.

When we are blocking this participation in life, we are of course blocking the satisfaction of our needs also. In fact, when we look at human needs, we find that there are two such needs which are usually not mentioned at all. First, as we are discovering already, we have the basic need to be aware of ourselves. Without this bodily awareness, we have an impossible time satisfying other interpersonal needs.

Secondly, we have the need to move! Our spirits rise up when we move. All primitive cultures know the essential value of dancing, for instance. There is an energy available for us, when we move, which otherwise lies dormant. This energy is our vitality, it is the essence of what makes us attractive to other people, and what makes us feel good in our bodies.

People who do not feel good in their bodies are the people who do not move adequately. Conversely, the people who are very much present in their bodies, who are attractive to others, and who feel wonderful in the present moment, are the movers!

Let's take a quick look at your movement habits.

1. Do you walk at least half an hour a day, or ride a bike, go jogging, swimming, etc.? Yes ___ No ___
2. Have you danced to your favourite music in the last week? ___
3. Do you prefer to remain seated than to get up and move? ___
4. Do you like to move your arms through the air? ___
5. If I suggest that you stand up and stretch right now, what is your reaction? ___
6. If I suggest that you go out for a walk right now and see who you might meet, what is your reaction? ___
7. If I suggest that you join an exercise programme, yoga, dance class, hiking club, what is your reaction? ___
8. Is movement a pleasure for you? ___

Simply start to notice your choices when it comes to moving, or remaining quiet and still. If you are a person who habitually avoids movement, begin to explore your feelings about movement. Risk a little and push yourself into going for walks, and see what bothers you in moving. You might discover certain anticipated problems in getting out and moving. Are these anticipations realistic, or simply old inhibitions left over from earlier days?

Of course, there will be many of you who do love to move, who keep yourself on the go all the time, who are so busy with your aerobic classes and your jogging schedules and such that you are completely avoiding the opposite need — to simply stop, to be quiet a few minutes, so that your soul can catch up with you and you can see yourself clearly. Many of us run away from ourselves through too much business, too much movement. If you are one of these people, so busy that you don't have time to stop and just look around you, you might be avoiding contact through never letting the dust settle.

One of my other teachers in past years, a philosopher named Alan Watts, was very intent upon my understanding the basic premise of his last years of life. He had determined that we live in a two hundred per cent universe, not a one hundred per cent universe. For instance, with movement and stillness, it is a hundred per cent true that movement is life, that your vitality comes through movement, and that movement is the key to a full life.

At the same time, it is a hundred per cent true that being still, remaining passive, stopping totally, is the key to a deeper lifestyle.

Each, in proper balance, seems best. We must move to find our new friend or partner. We must stop to recognize him or her. Then we must move together to remain together. So if you have a bad habit of not moving about much, you can act to move more; if you never hold still, start looking at this habit, and allow a quietness to come into you. In both cases, an awareness of your breathing, and your body is essential for success in growth.

THE ATTRACTION MEDITATIONS

We have now arrived at one of my favourite phases of 'finding each other'. Whether you are needing a parking spot, a new apartment, or a new friend, you can apply these basic principles to enhance your potential for success.

At this moment, you are sitting here reading this page, aware of your interpersonal frustrations and yearnings, and wondering if there is someone out there whom you will meet at some point in the future who will satisfy your needs.

At this very same moment, there might be one person out there in the world, or ten people, or even a thousand people, who have similar feelings to those you feel right now, and who in fact could form a satisfying relationship with you, if only you could somehow bring your two bodies to the same point on the planet at the same time.

This is the challenge. How do you make contact with a person of like mind to you? How does your physical body come into contact with a person 'out there' who is ready, and able, to share his or her life in some way with you?

Traditionally, people prayed to God for a partner. Often these prayers seemed to be answered. A magic seemed to work, suddenly to bring you together with a person whom you recognized somehow as the person you needed in your life.

Many of us have lost our belief in a fatherly God up there, who looks after us and sends us our bride or husband with his blessing, and perhaps it is pointless to argue one way or the other in this regard, but both my personal and my professional experience indicate that there is a certain magic in life, a magic which we cannot fully identify scientifically at this point, but which manifests itself regularly in the coming together of people throughout the world.

One thing appears certain: God helps those who also help themselves. This old aphorism directly reflects on the present programme. Only if you actively make efforts to work through your personal blocks and inhibitions will you optimize your opportunity for encountering a satisfying partner or friend. I am assuming that you have taken to heart the earlier exercises in this programme, and are moving into this realm of attraction meditations after reflecting upon the more cognitive and emotional aspects already presented.

There are two elements of this approach to consider. First of all, to what extent can you expand your consciousness so as to include another human being in your 'bubble'? Secondly, to what extent can you consciously attract a similar person towards you?

In the first element, we are dealing with your readiness to be together with someone new. Many of my more conservative colleagues feel that the attraction meditations are actually only psychological preparations for this expansion of one's personal world to include a new person. Even if this is all that happens, it is an invaluable step towards a new relationship.

Very often we enter into a relationship, we have problems with the relationship, it comes to an end and we experience considerable, often agonizing, emotional pains from the separation. When this happens, a person's 'bubble' contracts with the pain, and refuses to consider letting a new person come into his or her world, for fear of a repeat performance and more pain. Has this happened to you?

Many people yearn for a new friendship, a new intimacy, at a conscious level, feeling the natural human need for such interpersonal contact, but deep down a part of them is afraid to open up again, to risk a new love affair or friendship. This can also happen at a business level, where you trust someone as a partner, get cheated, and then refuse ever to trust anyone again in that way.

So let's begin with a simple exercise, and see how you do.

SHARING YOUR BUBBLE

All of us live in a bubble of consciousness. We are aware of ourselves, of our surroundings, and of the people we allow into our personal world. Beyond a certain point, we are not aware. We know the world is out there, because we have a concept of the world in our heads, but what we are directly aware of is limited to our consciousness. Most of us actively exclude from our bubble of awareness many negative things in the world.

This was especially evident to me when I was living in West Berlin, doing therapy with people in that little bubble of Western civilization, surrounded by antagonistic walls and barbed wire and emotional resentments.

My clients had almost all eliminated from their personal bubble of awareness the reality of the Communist world on the other side of the wall. They lived within their confines of family, work, recreation, and completely ignored the surrounding world on the other side of the Wall. In fact, when I was living there, I had extreme difficulties with certain expansion meditations, because after a few months I didn't want to deal with the 'outside world' all the time either.

If you have been hurt by the 'outside world' in a past relationship, do you now have your consciousness contracted so that there is no room for a new human being to come into your bubble?

Just reflect upon this without judgement.

Imagine right now that there is someone with you, with whom you have a deep relationship. Imagine that there is someone inside your bubble. How does it feel?

In fact, are you aware of your own physical presence in your bubble? This is very often lost also when there has been emotional pain in the past. People contract their bubble to exclude their own bodies, where the pain exists. They move into safe, but often neurotic, patterns where they are aware of their preferred concepts, their preferred projections, their preferred memories — but their own existence in the present moment is somehow outside their awareness.

Emotional healing, seen from this point of view, is actually a process of consciousness expansion to include the whole person in his or her own bubble of awareness. If you are having troubles with the simple consciousness expansion exercises of previous chapters, be gentle with yourself. You very possibly are needing to risk an expansion of your bubble to include dimensions you were hurt in, and have run away from. This takes time. Your only challenge is regularly to return to the exercises, and step by step to risk opening up again.

So let's do a particular meditation which directly aids in this expansion. After reading this description of the exercise as a whole, you can put the book aside and do the meditation.

Sit quietly, with your eyes closed. Focus first on your breathing, then on the force which seems to keep you breathing, when you make no effort to take your next inhaled breath. Allow your awareness of this natural breath reflex to expand, so that you can relax and rest assured that you continue breathing when you make no effort to breathe. This is a contact with your basic lifeforce, and to become aware of this regularly is immensely helpful. It will be with this lifeforce that you begin to expand your bubble of awareness.

Now be aware also of the air going in and out of your nose, so that your awareness includes your head. Expand your awareness so that you are conscious of the volume inside your head itself. Take your time, make no effort, simply point your attention in this expansive direction. See what experiences come to you when you do this now.

Once you are aware of your breathing, and the space inside your head, you can effortlessly expand your awareness to include your whole body at once, from your head to your toes. With every breath, observe how your awareness changes, grows, expands.

At this point, you are fully aware of yourself, but of no one else. See what happens when you allow your awareness to expand another step, to include the dimension of space around you.

Allow whatever feelings and emotions that want to come to the surface to be present at this point. Breathe into the feeling of your body existing in space. Feel the bubble that you live in, and allow it to expand as much as it wants to right now.

In this expanded state of awareness, see what happens when you open yourself to the possibility of having someone else being in your space. Don't conjure up an imaginary person, simply get a feeling for how ready you are to have a new person exist within your territory.

Do you still want to be alone in your bubble, or are you ready to share it with someone?

How close do you really want this person to be to you? How much space do you need to keep for yourself?

In doing this 'sharing your bubble' meditation, you can explore for yourself how you feel about letting someone into your private spaces. Each time you do the meditation, you will discover new feelings, new thoughts rising to the surface, and in this way, you can get to know your deeper needs, both for intimacy and sharing, and also for your own privacy and solitude. It takes both dimensions for a relationship to work.

SOMEONE OUT THERE

Now that you are beginning to get a feel for your own readiness to bring someone into your bubble, into your life in some way, we can turn again to consider the reality of a person our there who is, at some point, going to appear in your life.

The first step is for you to be open to the actual reality of this person. It is one thing to dream, to have fantasies of the ideal friend or mate. It is entirely different to shift from fantasies to reality. There is someone out there. At some point, you are going to see him or her for the first time.

In fact, right now, you can do a meditation and make contact with this person. The simple logic of physics indicates that this is possible. Consider the reality of the situation you and this person are in, right now. You are on a collision course. For you to meet in the future means that right now you are moving towards each other, you are on mutually attractive courses in life. Every step you

make is going to bring you closer to this person. It is only a matter of projection to sense your coming encounter, and thus to sense your relative positions right now!

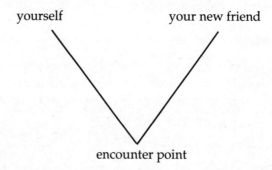

yourself   your new friend

encounter point

With this view of your relationship in mind, you can see that you exist in the other person's life already. So what would happen if you did a meditation in which you focused on this person's presence, in the present moment, before the encounter ever happens?

Just give it a try. I know this is a somewhat radical notion for many of you, so just play with the idea; you don't have to take it seriously, simply see what experiences you might have, when you consider this dimension of encounter. Make yourself comfortable, and turn your awareness to your breathing, as we have learned already. Expand your awareness to include your whole body at once. Then expand to include the space around you.

Now, effortlessly, with no fantasy images at all, allow your awareness to expand to feel the presence of your new friend on the planet with you, right now. He or she is here, somewhere, on the planet. Simply see what experience comes to you when you expand your awareness to include him or her in your bubble of awareness.

Be careful not to play games with yourself at this point, not to begin to fantasize, to create images and thoughts in your mind. This is not a thought/image/memory/fantasy game. This is a direct perception, an experience in the present moment, which will be completely new to you when you do it. So experience the present moment, hold your attention on your new friend out there, and *do nothing*! Only remain focused on the presence of your new friend.

At this point, it is essential that you don't try to manipulate the situation, that you don't have your will-power jump into the picture and try to force anything to happen. Remain passive, and feel what natural forces you encounter, which spontaneously create a field of attraction between you and your future partner, friend, comrade.

In talking with many couples who came together 'as if by magic', we have found that most of them were doing this meditation, naturally, before they met their partners. At a certain point in their lives, they had worked through the first stages we have been looking at, and they felt very good about themselves. They felt an expansive sense of their own presence, and at a certain point began to feel that there was in fact someone out there, someone they could sense even though they had not yet met.

As this feeling of the other person's presence became stronger, as they focused more and more on this dimension of their awareness, their vitality expanded also and they became like a magnet.

Then suddenly, at some moment in time, in the 'here and now' they both were living in, they saw each other, and that magic 'love at first sight' occurred.

85

Is this what you want to have happen?

Even if it is not romantic love you want, the same basic premise functions. Whatever your need is, you can begin to sense the person out there who can fulfil it.

Once you clearly know your needs, you can focus on the person who can fulfil those needs. Once you have gone through the emotional steps, the personality-expansion steps, the preparation for your encounter, you are ready to move actively forward to that encounter!

Even if you know that you have some growing to do before you are ready for your new relationship, you can begin to practise this 'attraction meditation'. Even if you are months or years from meeting this new friend, you are already on collision course, and you can feel the other person's presence when you do the meditation.

The beautiful thing about this meditation is this: once you feel the other person's presence, you can relax! In a deep sense, you no longer feel alone. You can expand your awareness to include this person, on deep levels, and feel a sense of communion which will deepen.

In our interviewing of 'love at first sight' couples, we found that this feeling of pre-encounter intimacy was almost always present. And at once the encounter had occurred, intimacy was so deep that there was no psychological explanation for the immediate feeling of oneness, of familiarity with the other person.

There are a number of explanations for such feelings, of course, and no one really knows how the magic works. All we know is that the basic 'attraction meditation' tunes you in to the magic, and with every meditation you do, you strengthen your potential for encountering the right person.

But I hope you can see that this final 'attraction meditation' is a culmination of the entire programme so far — it is the last step in the development of your sense of self-awareness, vitality, and self-love. I want to encourage you not to feel in a hurry to master this meditation. You have your natural growth rate, and if you remain in the present moment, enjoy yourself as you experience your current level of awareness, you will find a new sense of peace and contentment with whatever level of development you are at, in your movement towards the desired encounter.

In fact, the essential ingredient in this formula is 'enjoyment of the present moment'. If you aren't having a good time with the first exercise, none of the future ones will open up to you.

So let's take a good look at the evolution of your ability to succeed with this 'attraction meditation' and to generate your desired encounter. You can see where you are in this development, and regularly, using this following list, go through the entire progression, pausing to focus on the step where you begin to lose your self-awareness.

THE PREPARATION PROGRAMME AS A WHOLE

1. FEELING YOUR BASIC NEED

Be aware of where you feel the need in your body.
Notice how it affects your breathing.
Think clearly about the steps to fulfilling the need.

2. TALKING WITH A FRIEND

Express your need to someone you are close to.
Consider the first twelve questions in depth.

3. GIVING TO OTHERS

Reflect upon your readiness to give.
Look inward to see yourself honestly and clearly.

4. REFLECTING UPON YOUR PAST

Consider the seven questions about your childhood.
Play the various therapy games with yourself.
Look directly at your fears and inhibitions.

5. EMOTIONAL HEALING

Regularly give yourself time to discharge emotions.
Watch your breathing throughout each day.

6. ENHANCING YOUR PERSONAL PRESENCE

Watch your breathing.
Expand to be aware of your whole body at once.
Expand again to include the space and air around you.

7. SEEING WITH YOUR WHOLE BODY

Do the personal presence meditation.
Then allow your eyes to open.
'See everything at once.'

8. DEVELOPING PERSONAL POWER

Do the twelve exercises regularly.
Remember the rules for reducing anxiety.

9. BECOMING MORE ATTRACTIVE

Consider the four keys to attractiveness.
Become your own best friend.

10. LIVING IN THE PRESENT MOMENT

Watch your breathing.

Be aware of the moment-to-moment sensory experiences.
Do the Krishnamurti exercise often.

11. EXPANDING YOUR PERCEPTUAL ABILITIES

See with your body.
Breathe through the eyes.
Look without projecting.

12. MOVING MORE

Evaluate your movement habits.
Do the personal power movements.
Encourage yourself to move more.

Starting The Attraction Meditations

Once you have mastered the basic twelve exercises just listed, you will find the attraction meditations a natural next step. Even while you are still growing through the twelve exercises, you can practise with the attraction meditations, and begin to be aware of your future friend or partner out there in the world, also focusing on you perhaps!

The Actual Encounter

Now, once you feel confident of yourself with the above exercises, you can begin the actual physical movement towards meeting the person out there who is also looking for you.

We will devote the next section of the book to this process. Feel free to read through this new section, even if you haven't integrated the exercises into your daily life as yet. It is good to see the entire programme as a whole, and then to go back and begin with the actual exercises. There is no dogmatic structure to this programme; you can feel free to work with it as you like, once you have an overview of its logic and direction.

PART FIVE
The Successful Encounter

So far in this programme we have been looking primarily inwards, reflecting upon our mental, emotional, and behavioural qualities which either encourage or inhibit encounters. We have learned to expand our consciousness to attract a new friend to us, and we have enhanced our relationship with our own selves.

Now we are ready to begin the actual search for the person we desire to find and be with. We are going to start looking at the outside world with the eyes of a hunter.

At this point, can you honestly say to yourself, "Yes, I am hunting for someone special out there, I am actively searching to find what I need"?

This is where so many of us fail in the search. We are afraid to put ourselves on the line, to admit we are trying to find a special person to be with. Because we are afraid that we might fail in this search, we hesitate genuinely to commit ourselves to the search in the first place.

Your entire life is going to be affected when you meet the person you are looking for. Are you really willing to have your life go through an unpredictable change, through the influence of a new person in your life?

In a deep sense you are risking everything in your 'known world' when you open yourself to a completely new person in your life. This is one of the reasons we have been focusing on developing your sense of personal strength, before you make your desired contact. If you are weak at the moment of encounter, you will be pulled off-centre.

So let's begin on the right foot in this search. Let's take on the role of the warrior in traditional Indian terms. We need to go out into the unknown world, to find something which we require for survival. If we begin this search in the proper state of mind, we optimize our success.

THE WARRIOR'S PATH

When I propose to clients that they become warriors in order to meet their desired new friend or partner, many of them are at first confused. Especially with women, the dream of finding an ideal friend or mate is a very soft dream, which in no way resembles the path of a warrior.

But the reality of the world out there is quite different from youthful dreams of romance. In your searching for the desired person, you are going to come into contact with many less desirable people, as I am sure you already know. To hold your own against these people is one of the primary tricks of a successful adventure in finding your new friend.

In fact you are going on an adventure as you begin to explore the world in search of what you desire. If you look at your search in this light, it can become a positive feeling of challenge, of adventure!

You do not go on an adventure in the same state of mind that you sit at home and sip tea by the fireside. When you go on an adventure, you first prepare yourself as we have been doing up till now, and then you go out into the world with your personal power radiant, your goals clear, and your spirit deeply centred within you.

Perhaps the finest manual concerning the development of the warrior is the collected writings of Carlos Castaneda, who presents the traditional teachings of the Yaqui Indians on this subject. Especially in *Tales of Power* and *The Fire from Within*, the qualities of a successful warrior are clarified.

Of special note here is that the art of stalking, of searching for your new friend with clear intent and strength, consists of five main elements. The first is control, learning to stay centred deep within yourself, so that you don't act impulsively and unclearly. The second is discipline, learning as we have to develop your inner qualities before running out to satisfy your interpersonal needs.

The third element in stalking is forbearance, the ability to let time pass, to be patient, to find satisfaction in the present moment rather than always pushing towards your end goal. The fourth element deals with timing, knowing when to act, when the moment has come to put aside your patience and to reach out for what you want.

The fifth element is will. This does not mean 'will-power' in our normal sense of the word, but rather the personal power which we have been exploring already. This personal power enables you to tap into the magic dimensions of life, and to gain power from deep sources when you need it. And certainly, the time when you need the most personal power is when you do find someone who strongly attracts you!

I hope you can see at this point how the entire first half of the book has been helping in your development of these five essential elements of stalking, of successful hunting. The fact that we find such traditions of stalking throughout the world indicates that they are rooted in the nature of human beings. I have presented them as being part of present psychological concepts, but these concepts, when they are genuine, are rooted in a wisdom that certainly pre-dates Freud.

Another concept from the teachings of Don Juan and the Yaqui tradition is directly pertinent here. This has to do with the 'worthy opponent'. When you meet someone new in your life who strongly attracts you, you have met your new 'worthy opponent'. As you know from past relationships, there is a challenge inherent in your opening yourself to relating deeply with another human being. There is a danger as well as pleasure, and at every step in a new relationship, you can make a bad move and fall flat on your face.

The primary danger of a warrior, whether a warrior in love, business, or battle, is to be found in faulty perception of the world around him or her. Certainly in romance, this is the killer danger. If you see your lover very realistically, without projecting your ideal dreams and fantasies onto this person, then you are safe. But if you begin a relationship based on illusions, you are inevitably heading for disaster, because at some point the bubble of romance is going to pop, and you are going to find yourself lost in an unreal world, where your concepts of your lover do not match the real person.

So now as you go out into the world to find your new friend, partner, colleague, lover, whatever, you should take a good look at your readiness for the adventure.

My recommendation is that you begin with very simple stalking exercises. Get to know the feel of the search for a particular desired item, and build up confidence in your ability to maintain your centre while out in the world.

SEARCH AND FIND MISSIONS

Before taking the ultimate challenge of stalking your new friend, of encountering a powerful source of satisfaction, try this 'dry-run' exercise.

Instead of focusing on your interpersonal need, focus on a more simple need, something you have run out of in the kitchen. Whether it is butter or milk, onions or your favourite drink that you need, pause a moment before going to the shop, and focus on your need. Go through the same procedures as you would in feeling the need for a new friend, be clear in your thoughts, feel the need in your body, reflect on past experiences in finding this desired item.

Then bring yourself into direct contact with your will to go out and find the item. Bring your focus to your breathing and your whole body at once, and feel the space around you, where you will in fact find the item.

Now, when you go to the shop, see if you can go as a warrior, stalking this item. See if you can stay aware of your breathing and your body for the entire time you are on your way to the shop, and especially when you are in the shop, pause, get centred, and see if you can feel the presence of the desired item in the shop.

This might seem a foolish game, but once you play it you will understand its power. Notice your habits as you approach the desired item. Notice what your eyes do as you search for it. These are key insights into your stalking habits, which all of us sciously have developed.

And when you find yourself looking at the desired item, pause, breathe, be conscious of this item in your bubble of awareness, Then, quite consciously, with satisfaction in your success, reach for the item and take it.

Remain conscious of this item as you pay for it, and take it home. As you consume it, also remain conscious of the final fruits of your searching and finding mission.

Do this with many different items which you go out to find and obtain to satisfy your needs. Practise! Every time you do this, you will gain a new understanding of the deeper process you are participating in.

ENCOUNTERING KNOWN FRIENDS

The next step in this development has to do with your feeling a desire to see someone you already know, and the fulfilment of that desire.

The next time you feel like seeing someone, don't act unconsciously to make this rendezvous happen. First pause and clarify the nature of the desire. Explore your emotional feelings as well. Go through the list of stalking elements which we discussed before:

1.   'Control' — remaining centred, focused within;

2.   'Discipline' — consciously bringing your attention to the direct observation of the need;

3.   'Patience' — remaining in the present moment rather than getting lost in the future;

4.   'Timing' — feeling the right moment to phone, or to go and see your friend, so that you feel calm and centred in the act of encounter;

5.   'Will' — focusing on your personal power which can

bring about the desired encounter, and staying centred
in this inner power as you act.

Now as you go about finding your old friend, you can see how
these different elements determine your ability to generate an
encounter, at least with your known friends.

As you approach this person, remain especially aware of your
breathing, your feelings in your body, and your perception habits.
Especially when you come into eye-contact with this person,
notice what happens! Do you remain conscious and centred within
yourself, or do you still have the habit of losing your centre when
you look at someone?

This is an ideal moment to practise the fine art of 'seeing with
your body'. Rather than focusing on a point, you can look to see
your friend as a whole, and while looking, keep looking inward
also. Be ultimately selfish right at the moment of encounter. See
yourself clearly, remain aware of your feelings, and then expand
your awareness to include your friend.

You will find that a calmness comes into you when you look in
this manner. Instead of jumping into verbal worlds, you can relax
a bit, and just 'share space' with your friend. Sharing space is
something to practise also, and we should give some specific
suggestions for this.

SHARING SPACE WITH A FRIEND

You can explain to your friend about this programme, about
developing certain abilities, and suggest that you practise this
following exercise together. Hopefully, this friend is the same one
with whom you got together to talk over your needs in Part Two,
so this will simply be the next step.

First of all, tell your friend that you have just practised the art of
stalking, and have in fact found whom you were desiring to
encounter. This in itself is a beautiful thing to admit to someone —
that you desired to be with them, and went through the art of
stalking to find them, and that both of you are happy that you
played warrior and acted to fulfil your need. Conscious recogni-

is very important.

Now, see what happens if you stop talking, close your eyes, and sit together a few minutes, with both of you doing the consciousness expansion exercise so that you are, in fact, both conscious of the same space at the same time. You are sharing this space. How does it feel to share space with a friend consciously?

At some point, feel free to open your eyes, but don't look to see anything in particular. Stay conscious of your own inner presence, and slowly allow the external world to come into your internal world.

Finally, allow you eyes to focus on your friend, and see if you can maintain this focus while still remaining aware of your own breathing and body.

You will find that your friendship moves into unknown spaces when you do this exercise. How do you feel about this venture into the unknown? Be honest with yourself, and talk it over with your friend also. Is your relationship based on maintaining security in known ways of relating, or do you accept this friend as a 'worthy opponent' who can help you push into new experiences, new ways of relating?

Throughout this book, we have been talking about your search for a new friend, a new partner or colleague to satisfy your unfulfilled needs and desires. At this point, it is time to give a slight twist to this search. Perhaps the new friend you are looking for is someone you are already in contact with. Perhaps instead of seeing someone completely new who attracts you, you will see someone you already know, but see them in a new light, and suddenly feel a new attraction.

You will notice that we have been playing a great deal with your perception habits. This is essential for most of us, because our perception patterns have been strongly conditioned to function only in very limited ways. We perceive friends in stereotyped ways usually, and hold a fixed concept of who they are in our minds, failing to notice that they are growing and changing, and perhaps have suddenly grown into an awareness which matches our present needs.

I have seen this happen many, many times — two people know each other for months, even years, they work together, socialize together, know each other within a limited definition of relating.

Then suddenly, they look at each other and see each other in a totally new light. Their perceptions open up, and they feel they are seeing each other for the first time. And pow! The desired encounter has taken place, and the new person is present.

THE HUNT BEGINS

At a certain point in time, perhaps today, perhaps next week, perhaps in a month, you will feel a new energy inside you, an energy which tells you that you are ready to commit yourself to searching out your new friend. Perhaps you have already felt this commitment. It comes spontaneously when you know, deep down, that you are prepared for the challenge.

When you feel this certainty that you are ready to go out and find who you are looking for, you should relax and enjoy this feeling. If you feel impatient to get out and find your next 'worthy opponent', then perhaps you are not really ready. There should be no impatience. Instead, a strange sensation of calm should come over you, as if you have all the time in the world.

If this encounter is destined to occur anyway, there is no need to push to make it happen. You cannot predict when you will find your new friend. All you can do is actively begin the search, and remain calm, confident, and satisfied with the present moment.

You will find that you like yourself a great deal, when this feeling comes over you that the search has begun. You will enjoy the feeling of being a warrior, of being prepared for whatever comes, of having your personal power well-centred within you.

A warrior does not hunt twenty-four hours a day. There is a time for hunting, and a time for other things. In the Indian traditions, a warrior goes hunting only when he can feel the presence of what he is hunting for. This means that you should go hunting for your friend only when your awareness is expanded to where you can feel your friend's presence. When you do not feel this expanded state, it is not the time to be looking, it is a time to pull back, collect your personal power and assess your inner feelings.

A warrior goes out with certain weapons, with which to capture what he hunts for. What weapons are you hunting with? Please, don't think of weapons as necessarily negative tools. You are hunting for your friend, and your friend is hunting for you. This is a mutual-hunting game! Only if you both have tools with which to make contact with each other, can your mutual hunting reach a fulfilment.

When you walk out your door, how can you actually make contact with someone in the outside world? You can see the person, first of all. This is the primary tool with which you can reach out and touch someone, to gain their attention.

You can hear someone, and use your voice to be heard. This is an important tool also. To a lesser sense, you can smell someone and be smelled, and you of course can reach out physically and touch them.

In the normal world of the street, the underground, elevators, restaurants and business meetings, you will primarily use your eyes and your ears to make initial contact with someone.

The challenge at this point is that you don't know what you are looking for, in terms of a visual or auditory image. Your eyes are going to be used for a more subtle form of seeing, separate from the recognition of an already-known object. You are going to be looking with your whole body, to get a direct 'feel' for a person. You are going to take in a person 'as a whole' and allow yourself to be responsive on deep levels to the way this person's visual stimulus affects you.

We don't know how this level of perception works. All we know is that it has worked millions of times, throughout the world, and that it is a natural ability when the perception is open.

Whether your perception instantly 'recognizes' someone special or whether this recognition occurs over a period of time doesn't matter. What matters is that you should be sensitive to this particular type of recognition, and feel it with your whole body.

Your breathing will be hit strongly when you suddenly realize that you are looking at someone who could be the person you are searching for. With the recognition comes a jolt of excitement,

which can instantly turn into anxiety.

Anyone who says that there is no fear associated with a sudden encounter is fooling you. You are looking at a person who could totally transform your life, and this possibility of course carries a fear reaction. We desire change, we want someone new to come into our lives and fulfil our deeper needs — but we also are afraid of the changes that will come, because they are totally unpredictable.

This is a curious quality of human beings. We want our lives to remain constant, secure, predictable, and at the same time, we hunger for sudden change, for the unknown to come and transform us completely. To understand this conflict, to see it clearly and accept it, helps immensely in moving through the shock of recognition.

THE SHOCK OF RECOGNITION

When a desperate person is hunting for an essential item, and suddenly sees it, what happens? A great fear is generated, the fear of having found the needed item, and of perhaps not being able to get it. So the desperate person will act impulsively, with a total loss of centre, as if there is no time existing between the recognition of the desired object and the obtaining of that object.

The warrior, however, when he or she sees the desired person, will instantly pull back, regain a full sense of centredness, and allow time to exist between the stimulus and the response. When you suddenly see someone who strikes you strongly, you should put your focus directly to your breathing, so that anxiety does not grip it. Then you can expand to your whole body, and then expand to the space which you are sharing with this new person.

And that should be enough for the beginning. You can have eye contact. You can explore the feelings which arise. You can certainly act with movement, with talking, with more eye contact. But if you find that you are moving into a state of anxiety, stop everything! To become desperate is almost always to lose your cherished goal. Relationships that begin in desperation usually end very badly.

To overcome desperation, you must first have gone through the steps of preparation, so that you are already free of the 'desperation blues'. If you have become centred in yourself, if you have become your own best friend, you will not be a desperate person.

At the moment of encounter, however, this desperation can return. If it does, put to use your new habits of regaining your centre. Make yourself most important!

We come to the next old proverb which guides us through difficult moments.

"Give God a chance to say 'no'!"

Many times in your search, you will look and see someone, and feel something between you and this person, through the eye contact. In many cases, this person is in fact not the one you are looking for. Certain bells ring through the contact, but not really the right ones. Old 'playboy' ideals might be activated, for instance; but you are not looking for an ideal, you are looking for someone who touches you a lot deeper than just sexually.

Men, especially, have great difficulties in perceiving possible friends and mates, because there is so much visual conditioning in our culture which programmes us to respond sexually only to particular shapes and movements. It is a great challenge to let go the conditioned perception habits, and to look directly at new people, to see them for who they are, rather than for their similarities to the *Penthouse* ideal.

The best way to determine an ideal partner for you sexually, of course, is to take a good look at yourself in the mirror, and then to find someone who is basically similar to you in attractiveness, fitness, etc. Running after the ideal sexual partner when your own body is much less than ideal is ridiculous. People mate with people who are basically similar to themselves, for mating to work successfully.

So as you go out looking for a new friend, do your best to shift your seeing from your habitual patterns, to one of the patterns we have been learning in this programme. The best trick is 'seeing with your whole body', where you shift from the labelling perception of the head, to the 'feeling' perception of the heart.

You will be amazed at how differently people will respond to your looks, when you look at them in this way. People can feel instantly if you are 'appraising them', if you are looking at them to compare them with ideal images in your imagination. No one likes to be judged this way.

When you really look to see someone directly for who they are, as unique human beings, you begin to find people returning your glances more, responding to you, and looking to see if you might be a potential friend.

SOMEONE IS HUNTING YOU

You are looking for someone. You are looking into eyes, listening to voices, awaiting a deep feeling of recognition as you take in the people around you.

Other people are also looking. There are many hunters out there. Some of them are hunting for the same reasons you are. Many of them are hunting for different reasons. Some of them are looking for a quick sexual conquest. Some of them are looking for a financial sucker. Some of them are looking for another neurotic person to play neurotic games with. Some of them are unclear about what they are needing, they are hunting blindly, desperately, grabbing without clarity.

You perhaps already know how to read people's looks to see

what sort of hunting game they are playing. If you don't, if you have been avoiding eye contact all your life so as to avoid the hungry hunters altogether, it is time you started looking back at them, to gain a full picture of the world you are calling your hunting ground.

When you return someone's gaze, be sure that you are first centred strongly within yourself. This is the trick to resisting the unpleasant looks which abound in the public square. You can look, learn what there is to learn, and then hold your centre and carry on if you are not struck positively. Remember, if you don't look at all, you remain in fear. If you don't face a potential danger, if you turn your back on danger, you place yourself in much greater danger.

If you never look, you won't see that particular glance which is the one you have been looking for yourself. The energy which creates love at first sight, for instance, is the energy of two hunters who have their personal power highly activated, who broadcast this power stongly through the eyes. When two such people look at each other and feel a harmony in their looks, the magic flash occurs!

You might be a powerful warrior, you might be strong and centred and so on and so forth; but let's consider the other side of this tango. Are you willing to be hunted and found, yourself? Can you allow another person to hunt you, to find you, to recognize you and actively to pursue you?

Are you afraid of being hunted?

For a successful encounter to happen, both partners must be in the process of hunting. So if you are afraid of being hunted, you are not really open to an encounter. Certainly, most hunters are not to your liking, and you must protect yourself properly once you perceive a negative hunter. But when you perceive a hunter who wants you, and whom you want also, you must open yourself to being 'gotten'. It is always a mutual surrender and conquest, when two people come together. Otherwise, if the coming together is seduction rather than mutual surrender, no relationship exists except the conquered and the seducer.

You can look back to your experiences in the past, to see your usual habits in this regard. Do you always play the seducer, remaining the top dog and never allowing yourself to surrender to another person? Conversely, do you always play the weak, submissive one, forcing someone to seduce you in order to make contact with you? In either case, you are perpetuating a pattern which generates loneliness, not companionship.

THE BEAUTIFUL BATTLE

When two people meet and find each other attractive, there begins a great battle. Only if the opponents are equally matched will the battle result in a satisfactory relationship. In fact we really need to find someone of equal power, of equal awareness, if we are to relate successfully. Otherwise, there is a constant domination, and a constant fighting, which comes automatically when the two people are not matched well.

So when you meet someone, you will find yourself naturally pushing and pulling, testing the person's strengths and weaknesses, seeing if this person is strong enough to handle you, and yet soft enough not to constantly over-power you. As opposed to fighting on the battlefield, this is more like wrestling for fun. You can test a person's strengths, but you don't have to do that person harm if you are stronger.

The testing and wrestling goes on at many different levels, from sexual, physical, emotional, intellectual, to like-and-dislike games, habit and preference games. Step-by-step, you must find out if you are able to share space.

You can save a lot of wear and tear, and save time also, if you begin your encounter as honestly as possible. Most of us present as positive an image as we can to the outside world. We cover our seemingly 'bad sides' and accentuate our 'best sides' so as to be accepted.

If you are not honest in the beginning, you build a relationship based on false images, and at some point the illusions are going to fall — and the relationship with it.

HONESTY IN THE BEGINNING

So when you begin to relate with someone, from the very first moment you see them, don't play games or pretend to be someone you aren't. Right when you look in someone's eyes, see if you can let them see you for who you really are, let them look deeply into you and get a 'good feel' for you.

If you do this, the person can feel honest attraction or rejection, and so can you. If you both choose to make a step towards each other after this honest appraisal, you have made the first step successfully.

When you are first talking, notice if you are talking to impress the person, or talking with an honest self-importance. In the American Indian traditions, the greatest danger to a warrior is 'self-importance' of any kind. If you are trying to maintain an image of yourself that is not naturally a reflection of your deeper self, you are heading for disaster. If you fool someone into thinking that you are greater than you really are, you have created an illusion which will probably ruin your relationship in the long run.

In the short run, people are put off by this 'puffing up' attitude. Obviously, if you feel the need to appear superior, you feel inwardly inferior. If this is true in your case, just look at it. Accept it. By watching this habit at work day-by-day, you can see it begin to correct itself. It is an old habit, from early childhood, and you need to pay it much attention, without judging, to let it relax and go away, so you can shine through as your natural self.

Starting on the right foot is essential in relating. It is extremely difficult to get on the right foot later on if you begin wrong.

THE CRUEL ART OF SEDUCTION

You have perhaps noticed that so far in this discussion, I haven't given you even one good come-on line to use in picking up girls, or in scoring with the handsome guy down the hall from you.

Nor have I given you tips as to the best places in town to meet available executives or hungry models. Such books exist, and certainly, if that is your style, those books are for you.

What we are looking at here, is a completely different approach to encounter.

Consider the following situation which two people could find themselves in.

They have just seen each other for the first time. They both are immediately interested in each other. But they are also somewhat shy, and a little afraid to initiate any conversation.

In the traditional 'pick-up' approach, the guy should have twenty good lines on the tip of his tongue, with which to begin a conversation. This will move him away from his actual feelings of bashfulness, and give the girl the impression that he is suave, a master of social and sexual situations. If she is sharp, she will have a come-back for his beginning line, and they can play social games and perhaps move into a shallow beginning of whatever relationship might develop.

And they will have begun their relationship on the wrong foot, not being honest with each other from the start, about who they are and how they feel.

Consider what would happen if both of them had gone through the preparation for encounter described in this book, and were following the guidelines suggested.

They look at each other first of all, and feel an instant energy flash between them through the eye contact. Then, they both catch their breaths, return to their own centres and relax into the feeling of being very much in the present moment, not pushing the moment, simply allowing some time and space to exist.

In this state, they can be quite acutely aware of each other. They can feel how the other feels, they can look back into each other's eyes and see the honest interest.

At this point there is really no need to come up with a phoney excuse to start a conversation. They can see the interest in each other's eyes and they aren't about to just walk away from each other.

They can also see that the other is strong inside, even if there is the initial shyness. Krishnamurti, one of the fine old teachers about relationships, encourages people to nurture their shyness, to let people see it, because it is an indication that the spirit is alive and well inside, that there is a sensitivity inside which has not been buried under all the conditioning of childhood. To show someone your direct response to meeting them is the best gift you can give.

In our studies of first meetings between people, we found in fact that most enduring relationships began in this way, with a little shyness showing, and with a mutual feeling that something instantly existed between the two people, so that there was no compulsion to push into talking.

In a word, time existed, plenty of time. There was also an expanded feeling of space, of shared space, so that already, before words were spoken, there was a sense of involvement, of being together.

This moment of meeting is a magic moment. To spoil it by trying to manipulate the situation is foolish. Manipulation is a curious behaviour syndrome which we should look at a little closer, because so many of us use it as our means of relating.

When one person can play social games very smoothly, and dominates the beginning of an encounter, the scene is set for seduction. Usually in our culture, the man is the dominating person, playing upon a girl's emotions, leading her into feelings of interest and desire, playing her as one would play an instrument, to produce the desired responses.

In the end, if one uses seduction, manipulation, to gain the friendship, sexual favours, and companionship of a new acquaintance, there is a very empty feeling. Rather than two people remaining equally vulnerable, equally open to the creation of a unique relationship, one of the people has taken control, and provoked certain reactions which lead to a very shallow, one-sided, and dishonest situation.

People who seduce are people who are afraid of surrendering. They have to be in control all the time, because they are afraid of what would happen if they lost control.

It is better to learn to lose control.

THE TRUST FACTOR

As a psychologist, I am not supposed to include esoteric dimensions in my work, especially those dealing with faith in the universe and other such amorphous notions. But I am a psychologist second, and a human being first, so it seems appropriate at this point to say a final word about my observations regarding relationships.

Almost all of the successful relationships I have studied have included the following dimension which both parties agreed with — namely, that their coming together was meant to happen, that it was a fateful encounter which could not be stopped. Somehow, it was written in the stars that they would spend their moments together.

This feeling needs to be looked at closely, because if this perspective of encounter is accepted, many things become remarkably easier and less stressful.

We can ask the primary question at this point, a question which has been in the air from the beginning of our discussion: "Do you trust the universe to provide you with your basic human needs?"

We can separate human beings into those who do not trust the universe, and who fight for everything they get out of life, and those who do trust the universe, who participate in life with dynamic energy, but who accept what is given to them as a gift from the planet, rather than something they fought hard for and won all by themselves.

Most of the successful relaters we interviewed shared the feeling that their partner came to them as a gift. They felt thankful for this gift, and to the unseen forces which had brought them together.

Almost never did we come across a healthy, loving relationship where one of the partners felt he or she had cleverly manipulated the other into loving him or her.

So from the beginning you might want to reflect on your attitude towards life. Does the planet provide for you, or do you fight and steal whatever you can to survive? Do you accept what is given you, or do you resent what you do not receive?

Obviously, from the discussion in this book so far, you know that I am not suggesting that you can just sit back and expect the universe to drop new friends in your lap; but also, I am not suggesting that you can go out and grab what you want from life, and satisfy your basic needs through that approach to encounter.

If you are trying to force your will upon the world, to get what you want from it in whatever way possible, you will inevitably end up lonely. If you have a track record of such relating in your past, you can stop now, look honestly at your manipulation habits, and see through them to the insecurities underneath your surface. Then you can go back to the beginning of this programme and work your way gently through each step, so that you arrive at a point where you feel ready to go out and actively look for what you need, but also accept what you receive as a gift, as a natural evolution of your life on planet earth.

NOT JUMPING TOO SOON

My father had a saying that went like this: "Always say no to the first offer."

Once you begin your hunting, don't jump too eagerly into the first opportunity which develops. Right when you are feeling an expanding flow in your life, pause and take a breather for a moment, a day, a week, and let the world go by without working to make anything happen. After the day or week has gone by, look around you and see who still remains ready to relate with you.

By letting go, you can see who naturally stays by your side. If you meet someone, take a breather, and then find that your potential partner or lover has instantly disappeared with someone else, perhaps you have learned something about that person which it was best to learn as soon as possible!

You will know what is happening in your encounter by watching your breathing. You will either feel tense in your chest, anxious and pushing the situation, or you will feel expansive, relaxed, and powerful in your breathing, letting the situation evolve in its own good time.

If you are tense and anxious, turn your focus inward and practise the exercises which you have learned for just such a situation! Regain your own centre. Put yourself first, hold your own ground, and be ready to let the person go if you must be in a state of anxiety and stress to begin the relationship. If you can't take a good breath of air in the beginning of a relationship, chances are you won't be able to later on either.

And regularly, the first few days or weeks, insist on returning to your own solitary space. From the beginning, maintain your bubble of awareness as your own. Pull back and meditate on the situation, feel that your personal reality remains intact, separate from the new friend. If you fail to do this, you are in danger of going unconscious, of losing your own presence and existing only as the relationship exists. Then you are addicted to that relationship, because you feel you won't exist without your partner.

Talk with your new friend about this, be honest about these most important things, from the beginning, and the ending can be much more satisfying.

PART SIX
Enduring Relationships

So now you are together. You have found each other. What next?

We are born into civilizations which carry with them immense programmings on how human beings should relate with each other, especially in deep relationships. Both our emotional and our cultural inheritance predispose us to particular forms of relationships.

For the propagation of the species, we are well-endowed. The sex drive provides the magnetism which brings people together; and the primal yearnings for an intimate relationship like the one enjoyed with Mother tend to hold couples together when the sexual compulsion has been satisfied.

However, these traditional forms of relationship appear to reduce and inhibit one's personal awareness, one's opportunity to grow and evolve, to explore the vast potential in human relating.

I do not want to judge the old, habitual forms of relationships. I simply want to take a close look at them now, with you, so that we can see if you want this form of relating, or if there might be an alternative which you and your new friend can explore.

First of all, we can look at the positive aspects of the traditional, dependency relationship, and see why it has been so popular throughout the generations.

Obviously, for a woman it is very helpful to have a man around to provide for her if she becomes pregnant. There is no doubt that when babies are involved, an enduring bond between husband and wife is desirable.

Is this what you want to do in your new relationship? Have you talked about this?

Once again, we should return to the beginning of our discussion, and consider the list of questions which we began with.

Now that you have found each other, what needs do you feel as primary at this point?

You can see that this programme of dealing with your needs does not end when you have succeeded in satisfying your basic interpersonal yearnings. The same approach can be used throughout your life, applied to whatever predominant needs arise. If both of you feel the dominant desire to begin a family and have children, then you are well-matched to enter into that relationship.

The essential thing again is to be very clear about the actual emotional yearnings you feel, and especially the thoughts which are generating these emotional feelings. Through the simple meditation of looking inward, you can come to know what your desires are. You must be willing to look without preconditioning — look just to see what is there inside you at this point.

First of all, let's consider the basic nature of being together with someone, and encourage honest discussion of these factors.

SPACE AND DISTANCE

Some people, when they find the ideal person they were searching for, want to be with that person all the time. What are your feelings now?

What about your own space? Do you want to lose yourself totally in your new relationship, or do you want to preserve a certain distance, a special dimension of your life which is still yours alone?

Are you afraid to step back from your new relationship, afraid that you will lose your new friend if you have your own solitary space also?

Talk this over with your friend honestly.

What does your friend need?

Communication is obviously the key word in this final discussion. If there is a subject which I mention here, which you are afraid to talk over with your friend, take a very close look at that fear. It is the poison which will erode your relationship if it is not dealt with.

Traditionally, couples were encouraged to lose themselves in each other. This was the biblical model, for instance, that two people come together and become one. As a youthful fantasy, this is a beautiful romantic dream, but what happens when you play into it?

As you grow up in your family, you go from your total oneness with your mother before birth, to a beginning sensation of solitary existence after the umbilical cord is cut. Then you have years during which you progressively are pushed into your own solitary spaces. You have your own crib, your own bed, then your own bedroom perhaps. You do not desire this isolation, it is forced upon you.

You also lose the physical intimacy with your mother. At first you are against her skin, you suck her breasts, you feel her loving closeness. In fact, it appears that infants see the entire universe around them as part of their own consciousness, with the mother included as part of them.

Then step-by-step, this is lost. You are forced to face the fact that you are a separate being from your mother. The older you become, the more separate you are, until, by the age of ten or twelve, you live in your own world.

Then comes the sexual energy into your body, the strong craving for a new union with another human being. This new union is in many ways quite similar to your old union with your mother, and in fact those old baby feelings are at the heart of 'puppy love'.

Once you find someone with whom to share this new intimacy, your old feelings of possessiveness rise up again. You have found a substitute mother, and you are determined not to lose her this time. You have that feeling of intimacy you had as a baby, and life is bliss again.

At this point, you can slip into the traditional form of a relationship, if it is a sexual bonding. You can lose yourself in this relationship, have children, become the mother or provider, and continue with this relationship throughout your life.

If you do so with a sense of your own separate space also, fine.

The difficulty comes if you go unconscious and become dependent on this other person for your very sense of self. You will find a security in this relationship, but you will also generate the anxiety of losing your loved one, and of being totally lost and alone.

It seems that the most advisable relationship these days is that which includes a sense of oneness, with a sense of individuality. You are both going to continue to grow together, but you must reserve space for your own unique growth, which will certainly be at least somewhat different from your mate.

You can see at this point the danger in losing yourself in a relationship. If you grow only in the same ways as your partner, you are limiting your personal growth considerably, because no two people grow in identical ways.

Especially in our modern world where divorces are so common, it seems that a beginning understanding that you reserve your space to grow independently can reduce the possibility that you will have to leave your partner completely after years of no freedom to grow at all. What do you think?

The beginning weeks and months of a relationship, no matter what its nature, are crucial in determining the later direction of that relationship. If you establish habits and understandings unconsciously in the first period of your relationship, you are going to be victim to those habits later on.

So how can you consciously begin your relationship? You can risk, right from the beginning, the loss of your new friend. You can put aside your attempts to please this person, and simply express your own needs as they arise.

To do this, you must remain aware of your changing needs! And to do *this*, you will need to set aside your own space, your own solitary time, to reflect, meditate upon the basic questions we began this book with, and to become clear in your own mind what you want next in life.

Also, you will need a partner who is willing to do this also, so that there is regular two-way communication.

Are you willing to risk losing your new friend, in order to be honest?

OTHER RELATIONSHIPS

For instance, once you have found a main friend who satisfies many of your pressing desires and hungers, do you drop your old friends and relationships, and just fixate on your new friend? Are you in the process of doing this now as you begin your new friendship?

This is a primary stumbling block for many relationships. You retreat into your friendship, engrossed in the intensity of your togetherness. You try to be all things to each other, to satisfy all the other person's needs yourself.

This is, of course, next to impossible.

So are you willing to risk losing your new friend, through being honest and admitting that you need to see your other friends also? Are you even willing to admit to yourself that your new friend is not totally satisfying all your needs?

Once again, look to your relationship with your mother. Sigmund Freud was not a god in his view of human relationships, but the fellow was absolutely accurate in many of his insights, and it is certainly true that much of adult behaviour is rooted in our infant experiences. Your mother, for instance, did satisfy all your basic needs in your beginning months of life. So, naturally, when you find someone with whom you can feel almost as intimate as you felt with your mother, you are going to expect this person to satisfy all your needs also. This is of course more critical for a man than a woman, but it applies in both directions.

Also, what about jealousy? Another infant emotion, this fear of losing your intimate to someone else. Can you risk letting your new friend go off to be with other friends? Are you two hanging out together all the time, simply through fear of losing each other?

I know this is very basic information which I am covering at this point; we all know these truths in principle, but even the most intelligent of us tends to forget the basics when love clouds our emotions and jealousy becomes an unexpected bedmate in a new relationship. Obviously, you are reading this book now, so you can share these thoughts with your new friend, and directly look to make sure you are not slipping into troubled waters in your beginnings.

If you find that such emotions as possessiveness and jealousy are clouding your relationship, the direct step to deal with them is through simply talking over your feelings, being totally honest even if it is embarrassing. All of us, myself included, slip into these feelings at certain times, and it is an act of a warrior to move through them, to face directly what scares you, to look at it for what it is, and to grow through it.

THE WARRIOR COUPLE

Finding each other was not the ultimate challenge. Relating honestly and creatively is the final challenge, which is ongoing and continually new. So you might discuss between the two of you whether you both accept this challenge of remaining honest, remaining true to your changing needs, and remaining centred in

your personal private awareness which continues, even though you are now together.

I hope you understand by now that I do not have an ideal concept of how couples should relate. Every relationship is unique, and every moment of a relationship is new. Never before has your relationship existed on the planet; you are exploring totally new possibilities together. This is the challenge which requires the warrior strength and openness. There will be times when both of you must be very strong, must fight to hold your individual centre, or you are both lost.

I have been talking about intimate sexual relationships just now, but the same applies in whatever relationship you are developing with your new friend. Do you keep your space? Do you communicate your needs honestly? Do you accept the challenge of continually letting the known relationship die, so that a new moment of relating can be born?

Being willing to do battle with each other seems a very unfriendly notion of friendship. When two different people come together, their differences naturally tend to pull the other person off-balance. Without the fighting, the individual differences are ignored, go unconscious, and they go to work to undermine the relationship.

Look back to past relationships. How well did you manage to hold your centre in the old days? What were your problems in the relationship? Are you getting set to repeat old errors in relating? Do you want to sink into an unconscious relationship at this point, or is the challenge of remaining aware of your individual centre one which you now want to take on?

SECURITY VERSUS FREEDOM

All of us would like a secure relationship. Worrying about our partner leaving us in the future is a great anxiety. We lost our mother's intimacy as infants, and we don't want to go through that pain of separation again. So what can we do to ensure that our friend will never desert us?

If we totally kill ourselves to newness, to change, to personal growth, we can gain some semblance of security. But even then, our friend might go and die on us, leaving us alone. There really is no security, so why do we struggle to gain the fantasy of security?

The path I am suggesting, as an alternative to the security/ dependancy game, is the path of maintaining your own personal power intact as a separate being, from the very beginning of a relationship. This is a difficult path, but it seems the only acceptable alternative to going unconscious in a deadening dependency relationship.

In fact, ultimately, this is the path we must choose anyway. We must learn to face our solitary pathway which leads to the ultimate solitary moment, death.

If we accept that we are going to die, we can accept that a relationship could die as well; but if we are, deep down, blocking our awareness of our coming death, we will also block any acceptance that our cherished relationship could come to an end.

A warrior develops a special relationship with his coming death. He learns to accept his death as his best friend and adviser, instead of seeing his coming death as his enemy. By accepting that any moment could be the last moment, the warrior learns the final value of living in the present moment.

The future might never come. The past is just a goodbye. So what are we left with, really?

We are left with the beauty of the present love, which came to us as a gift and can leave us at any moment just as it came.

Once again, we return to our basic expansion exercise, which brings us into the present moment. All of our worries about losing our loved one are actually nothing more than thoughts, right? Our thoughts about the future generate the emotional responses in the body, and cause us suffering. Do those thoughts really accomplish anything? For all our worrying, for all our begging our loved one to promise to be true for ever — still our loved one could get hit by a truck tomorrow and that would be the end of it anyway.

So best to return to the breathing and the body, the space you are sharing right now, and enjoy it!

121

YOUR IMAGE OF YOUR LOVED ONE

Whether your new friend is a tennis partner and business associate, a spiritual guide or a lover, you will want to be careful that you don't develop in your mind an image of this person which remains fixed even though the real person is continually growing and changing. We tend to establish an idea, a concept, of who a person is, and if this concept becomes out of date, it will interfere with your direct relating with this person.

If you look with just your head, with your concepts, at this person, you will indeed develop a rigid picture of who your friend is. But if you look with your whole body, regularly, you can maintain this person as a growing, new being, always surprising you with his or her freshness.

A fine exercise to do together is to sit quietly for five minutes, a few feet from each other, looking at each other. Let your faces be relaxed with no expression, and first turn inward to your breathing and your body. Then see your friend's face 'at once', looking to see the whole face rather than details of it.

As you remain aware of your breathing and continue staring at your friend, you will notice that your eyes begin to play tricks with you. Allow this to happen. You will see your friend's face turn into another face perhaps, into mythic monsters, beauties, whatever your unconscious wants to play with at the time. As you allow your unconscious to play in this way, you can see all the unconscious images you hold of your friend in your mind, which are right below the surface all the time.

I recommend that you don't analyse these images, or even talk about them very much. Simply let this visual play occur, enjoy it, and then let go of it. But if you do this once a week, you will find continual changes in the nature of your hallucinations. Sometimes, there will be no changes at all, you will simply see your partner's face. Sometimes there will be total hallucinations. Just allow the process to continue until you both want to stop the session.

You can also do this exercise with yourself, in the mirror. See what changes happen when you look at yourself, and accept them.

I highly recommend that you take a very light attitude towards this playing. People get lost in analysis of these images, and to indulge in such mental games seems mostly fruitless. There are better things to do, such as remaining in the present moment and carrying on with life!

LEAVING EACH OTHER

Sometimes, relationships come to an end. This is not necessarily a tragedy. It simply means that you have given to each other what you had to give, at least in the present, and you now have other needs which need fulfilling, which require either solitude, or a new intimate partner. Our needs change. There is nothing we can do about this. Sometimes a relationship lasts a lifetime effortlessly. Other times, it is here today, gone tomorrow. Letting go gracefully is perhaps one of the greatest challenges.

You will have to pull back strongly into your personal centre. You will also need to release whatever emotional pressure is building up inside you. Baby feelings are natural at this point, and releasing them is the only healthy means of being free of them.

If you have maintained your private centre throughout the relationship, letting go will not be as difficult, as it would be if you had lost your centre in the other person.

Joel Kramer, in his priceless book of discussions called *ThePassionate Mind*, speaks very directly to the changing nature of love. Love comes and goes, we have no control over it, it is a wild thing, free to do what it wants. It is also a blessing which we can enjoy while it is with us, and which we must surrender when it goes.

All too often, we demand that someone love us all the time. In making this demand, we violate the nature of love. We force the other person to pretend to a feeling that is not always there. But if we accept that love is a free spirit, not an obligatory state, we can accept our friend's changing feelings. If we regularly accept that our friend does not have a flow of love for us at times, and feel this separation, then we are not afraid if the love leaves for a longer period. We also find that our own love for our friend comes and goes, as it wills. When we are not in the direct love experience with our friend, do we feel guilty?

Talk this over with your friend. Get clear about the flow of love between you, and the unspoken obligations you might be pressing on each other. Also get free of the guilt feelings that come when you look and find that, in the moment, the love is only a memory, not a present feeling.

In this way, your relationship can evolve to beautiful places you have never been before with another human being. If you risk all, you gain all!

Another factor in love to remember is that sometimes it seems gone not only for moments, but for days, even weeks. Sometimes people are even apart from each other for years, and then find that their need for each other has returned, and they come together again; but only if you let go gracefully can you leave doors open for a new return in the future.

FINAL WORDS

We have now looked at the entire process of 'finding each other', from the beginning feelings of yearning for someone, through the preparation stages for the mutual hunt, then the hunt itself, the encounter, the development of the relationship, and hopefully the enduring of the friendship.

Now that you have read through this description of the process as a whole, you can return to wherever you personally need to focus. Hopefully, you can carry on to succeed with your desires and deeper interpersonal needs.

To end this discussion, I would like to return to where we started, with that feeling inside you which motivates you to reach out and find someone special. This feeling of a need is the essential ingredient in all relationships, and as such should share our final attention.

Our instincts for human intimacy and compassion, for desiring to share our lives with other people and to work together for mutual satisfaction, are a complex intermingling of genetic programming and childhood conditioning. As such, they form a primary base for all our sophisticated ways of thinking and acting.

These instincts are both our motivation for 'finding each other', and also, if we are not careful, our tragic downfall in relationships. The deep yearnings are our human inheritance, and as such they underlie all our struggles to gain a successful interpersonal lifestyle. But the programmed patterns can also, as we have seen in this conversation, force us into states of emotional dependency which seriously limit our growth and satisfaction.

The challenge of growing into new forms of relating, where we are not victims of the unconscious relationship habits of our culture, is certainly the primary theme of this book. We are living in times when traditional forms of relating are breaking down rapidly. We all face the choice of slipping back into the secure childhood feelings which used to glue most relationships together, or of moving forward into the exploration of new union possibilities.

Naturally, we cannot put aside our cultural programming and leap into totally new states of mind and heart. As Joel Kramer says in perhaps the best book on the theme, *The Passionate Mind*, 'We cannot run away from our conditioning; we are our conditioning. In fact, creative new movement does not come from negating the old, but rather moves onward from it.'

This is why we have been developing, through this programme, a heightened ability to look directly at ourselves, directly at our conditioning and mostly unconscious habits of relating, so that we can see our base, and grow step-by-step beyond that base.

We can do this on our own, alone, to a considerable extent, but there are certain dimensions of human growth which require interaction with others. Our natural ability to let our love flow from us to another person, and to receive another person's love in exchange, is a human potential which we must develop together with another person.

I have not discussed the phenomenon of love directly in this conversation so far, but I am sure you have been aware of its pervasive influence on all that has been said. Love is an energy which underlies the growth of all relationships, and the exercises we have been exploring are all aimed at increasing your capacity to give and to receive this magical substance called love.

Love is expansion, just as hatred is contraction. Love generates an increased state of consciousness, when it is true love; but when possessiveness, jealousy, and the compulsion towards security contaminate love in a relationship, the love quickly goes, and anxiety, as we have seen, takes its place.

So as you move into your new relationship, I hope you can take seriously the challenge of remaining conscious and expansive, centred within yourself, as you form the patterns of your new friendship. You are acting out the basic human ritual in this act of creating a new relationship. Our human potential on the planet depends on each of us growing into new forms of relating which reflect the newly evolved situations we now find ourselves in.

In fact, it seems that the entire human species is undergoing growing pains, especially when it comes to forming successful relationships. Every time two people come together, there is the chance of a leap forward in our evolution, as a completely unique and dynamic relationship emerges. Certainly, when we look around us, we can see that great leaps are required in our evolution on subtle levels, if we are to keep the fabric of our civilizations from unravelling.

When I was quite young, I used to sit and listen to the Indian neighbours talking about the problems of the 'white man'. For the Indians, the white men (and women) have one fatal flaw — they think with their heads, instead of with their hearts, and therefore are capable of atrocious acts against the planet itself, from which all life springs. I remember feeling very guilty for having somehow been born into a civilization which could be seen in such a light.

We all have the potential to move deeply into our bodies and hearts in our thoughts and actions, if we can succeed in finding our own centre, in breathing into that centre, and allowing spontaneous thoughts to rise from our depths — and in acting on those deeper impulses.

So I especially recommend that you turn your attention regularly to the consciousness expansion exercises in this programme, which will serve as your base in all interpersonal challenges. I suggest this not just as a therapist who knows the therapeutic value of the exercises, but also as a person who does these exercises regularly himself, in order to continue with personal growth and expansion.

In fact, this programme is not simply aimed at the one-time attainment of a primary friend or mate. Throughout our lifetime new needs appear, often quite unexpectedly, and press us into action to satisfy them.

In my own life, I also find the basic techniques effective in enhancing my ability to find all things which I develop a need for, including a new house to live in, a new restaurant to explore, or even a parking place downtown. When I become clear of the need I feel in my body, and expand my awareness to include the existence of the desired person or thing out there in the world, my hunting is much more successful.

In writing this book, I am hoping for the same for you in your life. May you have enjoyable preparations for your hunting, a good amount of magic in your encounters, and much loving as the new days appear!

A REVIEW OF THE 'FINDING EACH OTHER' PROGRAMMES

Now that you have read through the book, you can return and go through the basic process outlined below for dealing with any of your interpersonal needs. After you become familiar with these steps, you will find that you can move through many of them quite quickly, and pause to spend more time where you feel the need.

1. **FEELING YOUR BASIC NEED**
   Be aware of where you feel the need in your body.
   Notice how it affects your breathing.
   Think clearly about the steps to fulfilling the need.

2. **TALKING WITH A FRIEND**
   Express your need to someone you are close to.
   Consider the first twelve questions in depth.

3. **GIVING TO OTHERS**
   Reflect upon your readiness to give.
   Look inward to see yourself honestly and clearly.

4. **REFLECTING UPON YOUR PAST**
   Consider the seven questions about your childhood.

5. **PLAYING THERAPY GAMES**
   Review the various games presented.
   Look directly at your fears and inhibitions.

6. **EMOTIONAL HEALING**
   Regularly give yourself time to discharge emotions.
   Watch your breathing throughout each day.

7. **ENHANCING YOUR PERSONAL PRESENCE**
   Watch your breathing first.
   Expand to be aware of your whole body also.
   Expand again to include the space around you.

8. **SEEING WITH YOUR WHOLE BODY**
   Do the personal presence exercise first.
   Then allow your eyes to open slowly.
   'See everything at once' as described in the text.

9. **DEVELOPING PERSONAL POWER**
   Do the twelve exercises regularly.
   Remember the rules for reducing anxiety.

10. **BECOMING MORE ATTRACTIVE**
    Review the four keys to attractiveness.

11. **LIVING IN THE PRESENT MOMENT**
    Focus on moment-to-moment sensory experience.
    Do the Krishnamurti exercise often.

12. **EXPANDING YOUR PERCEPTUAL ABILITIES**
    See with your body.
    Breathe through the eyes.
    Look without projecting.

13. **MOVING MORE**
    Look often in the 'movement mode' of seeing.
    Evaluate your recent movement habits.
    Do the personal power movements.
    Encourage yourself to get out and move more.

14. **THE ATTRACTION MEDITATIONS**
    Share your bubble.
    Focus on your new friend's presence.

15. **THE SUCCESSFUL ENCOUNTER**
    Search and find missions.
    Encountering known friends.
    Proper hunting procedures.
    Remaining centred during the encounter.